Faith
Connections

Leader's Guide

Spring
23

Four World-Changing Days
The Message of James
The Holy Spirit

Leader's Guide

Contents
Spring 2023
VOLUME 46, NUMBER 3

FoundryLeader.com

To enhance your session preparation, check out the following resources available online

Leader's Guide

•**Unit Videos:** All new videos by biblical schol and leaders now available on FoundryLeader.com. As a leader, gain insight and suppo from the expertise of leading Wesleyan scholars. This quarter Dr. Roger Hahn intro duces Unit 1, 2, and 3.

•Editable versions of the session so you ca customize to fit your unique group situatic

•Session notes that enable the group to fo low the discussion questions.

•PowerPoints for each session.

Illustrated Bible Life

•**Articles Out Loud:** Don't have time to read th *Illustrated Bible Life* article for the week? Yo can now listen to the article on the go with the new, weekly IBL "Articles Out Loud."

•Articles and verse-by-verse commentary f each session.

Access the materials on FoundryLeader.co using a password obtained by the purchas of the *Leader's Guide* and/or *Illustrated Bibl Life.* There is a separate password for each listed in your material.

Leader's Guide is published quarterly by The Found Publishing®, P.O. Box 419527, Kansas City, MO 641 Copyright © 2023 by The Foundry Publishing®. Canadian GST No. R129017471.

See page 86 for additional copyright informatio

Perspectives

Relationships

One of the greatest treasures people can possess is a meaningful relationship with another. I am not talking about a superficial relationship, but one that is built to last. What are the keys to a valuable relationship? First, there is the trust factor. You can put your faith in each other regardless of the circumstance. Second, each of you has the other's best interest in mind. Both of you would never intentionally do anything that would harm or hurt the other. Third, both of you are willing to go the extra mile for the other. The decision to go above and beyond the call of duty is never in question. Finally, the most important key is that the relationship is built on a foundation of (authentic and selfless) love. Love is the key!

In the first unit of this quarter we will examine the Passion Week to discover the relationship Jesus was sent to establish with us through His life, death, and resurrection. God loved the world so much that He sent His Son, Jesus, to die and rise again so that victory over sin and death is possible for those who place their faith in Him. That is, Jesus lived, died, and rose again so that people could be brought into a right relationship with God. That is the message of Easter. That is the good news of the gospel!

God not only wants us to be in a right relationship with Him, He also wants us to be in right relationship with others. This means allowing the Holy Spirit to guide us in the things we say and do. This means seeing others as God does and loving others as Christ would. Although we cannot control the thoughts, words, and actions of others, we can allow God's Spirit to guide our thoughts, words, and actions so that we are being Christlike in all our relationships.

Throughout this quarter, consider what it means to be in a right relationship with God, as well as, think about what it means to "live a life filled with love, following the example of Christ" (Ephesians 5:2, NLT) in your relationship with others.

May God bless you as you study His Word this quarter!

MIKE WONCH
Editor

Questions?

● Call our toll-free teacher help line, 1-877-386-0882, Monday—Friday, 8:00 am—4:30 pm.

● Email us through "Ask the Editor" on our website FoundryLeader.com.

● Write us at P.O. Box 419527, Kansas City, MO 64141.

Prepare to Lead

What You Will Find in a Typical Session

Session Outcome: The session objective for that particular session.

The Word (Scripture focus): The Bible study for each week is based on Bible verses (NIV translation) printed in the session.

Key Verse: Each week a key verse of Scripture is highlighted. This verse (or verses) points to the theme of that week's session.

Session Theme: The underlying theme of each session is captured in a single sentence and presented as the session truth.

Engage the Word: The Scripture exposition represents an in-depth, practical examination and explanation of the Scripture passage.

Discussion Guide in Four Steps

Connect to My Experience (Opening activity to introduce the session.) This opening is designed to capture their attention and interest, and begin to move their thoughts to the Bible study topic.

Connect to the Word (Reading and unpacking of the Scripture passage.)This is the time when you "unpack" the session passage and understand what the message of the verses has to say to us today.

Connect to My Life and the World (Heart and life connections to the biblical passage and steps to apply the Word in daily life.) Discussion on how today's session relates to life and ways to involve the adults in making personal decisions and commitments to enact God's Word in their lives.

Insight This is information that will help you as the facilitator understand the session passage in a deeper and more comprehensive way.

Unit 1 Introduction

The New Creation Burst Forth in the Death and Resurrection of Jesus

The death and resurrection of Jesus Christ is the very foundation of the Christian faith. It is the good news! It is the cornerstone and first fruits of the Triune God's work to heal and redeem all humanity as part of the new creation that is heaven coming to earth. It is God's declaration that sin and death do not have the final word. It is the hope for the world!

Within the good news of Jesus Christ's death and resurrection there are some important aspects of this celebration that can provide a more robust hope and transformation in love. We must not sanitize the shock and horror of Jesus' death; we must remember that the death is only salvific because of the resurrection; we must not neglect the fullness of Jesus' life and ministry; and we must remember that to fully receive the gift of salvation we must also take up our cross and follow Christ.

Horror and Despair of the Cross

As a child growing up in the church, I learned early that Jesus died on the cross for my sins. This was believed without question or hesitation. While I still affirm this today, because I am so familiar with this story there is a danger that I neglect the shock and horror of the event. While it is true the Gospels record Jesus announcing His upcoming death (Mark 8:31-33; 9:30-32; 10:32-34), it is clear from Gethsemane forward that the death of Jesus was unimaginable to the disciples. The disciples are fighting with swords, fleeing in fear, and denying they even know Jesus to servant girls. The despair of that first Good Friday and Holy Saturday must not be sentimentally glossed over. They knew His death meant it was all over. Hope, life, and faith are dead and eviscerated into the abyss. To those with earthly empire imagination, His death was clearly viewed as a sign that Jesus was a liar and the kingdom and God He was preaching about was false. In their minds, if Jesus was the Messiah, there is no way God would let Him die, and especially die a cursed death. Moreover, Christ himself cries out in pain and despair with the Psalm 22 lament, "My God, my God, why have you forsaken me?!" Jürgen Moltmann reminds us that on the cross the Father abandons Jesus and does not rescue Him from this evil death.* In Jesus, God becomes the God of those who have been abandoned and forsaken. We also must remember that not only does Jesus die and suffer the death as a Son, God the Father suffers the death of God's Son all in, by, and through the power of the Spirit.

This is one of the great blessings of a Tenebrae (service of shadows) service on Good Friday. This service reminds us both of the horror of Jesus' death and our culpability to it. I often offer a short refrain on Good Friday on social media "He is dead, and we have killed." Moreover, the entire season of Lent form Ash Wednesday to the Passion Week are gifts for the church to remember our sinfulness, our mortality, along with the invitation to follow Jesus into the shadow of the cross. Without considering the horror and despair of His death, we will miss out on the unimaginable joy of Easter.

Resurrection Needed

As I grew up, I began to question a bit more the central claim that Jesus died on the cross to forgive our sins. So how did this work? Is the cross more for us or God? Is killing Jesus good or evil? Did God want or need Jesus to be killed to love and forgive us? While some of these questions still leave me in mystery and wonder, I was given general answers that seemed to fall in line with what I later learned are largely substitutionary atonement theories. (By the way it is important to note that the Christian tradition has celebrated five to eight major atonement theories and has never settled on just one.) While there are several theories that circle the substitutionary orbit, the general sense was the Jesus died to pay a legal debt or restore God's honor. What became striking about these answers is that many of them seemed to neglect the need for the resurrection. During Bible quizzing I was struck by I Corinthians 15:17, "If Christ hasn't been raised, then your faith is worthless; you are still in your sins" (CEB). Any conversation on the atonement or salvation that neglects the resurrection is incomplete. Also, in 1 Corinthians 15:20, Paul celebrates that Christ is the first fruits of those who will be raised. Christ's resurrection in the full launch and inauguration of the kingdom of God on earth and the beginning of the New Creation coming to earth in the renewal and redemption of all things.

It is also important to celebrate that in the Father's resurrection of Jesus by the Spirit, this is not a reversal of His death. One of the powerful parts of the resurrection narratives with the disciples was that they can see and touch His wounds. This is the resurrection of the crucified God. The great news of the resurrection is that death and sin have been defeated. As Christians, we can also join in this resurrection life (1 Corinthians 15:22). This resurrected Christ still has a body with mutilated flesh, a continual reminder that it is in and through His stripes we find healing (Isaiah 53:5).

Just as there is a danger of emphasizing the death at the exclusion of the resurrection, there is also the danger of celebrating the joy of Easter without the pain and sacrificial obedience of Christ's death. With only the death there is no hope, with only the resurrection there is a failure to see the destructiveness of sin.

The Full Incarnation

As I continued my Christian discipleship, I observed in Christian preaching that the death and resurrection were being celebrated and focused on almost to the exclusion of everything else. I was struck with several Christmas sermons that were focused on the joy of Jesus coming to die on a cross. Is that all that really mattered? Is the salvation offered through Christ really only about the last 36 hours beginning with His death and stopping at His resurrection? Is Christmas really only about joy coming to earth so Jesus can die? Not only was Christmas becoming hijacked by Christ's death and resurrection, I also observed how Jesus' life and teachings were seen as nice and kind, but not central to the "real" part of salvation. During my theological training I learned about the great eastern parts of the Christian faith. One of the great gifts of the eastern Christian tradition is the importance of Christmas. As the early church debated about how to celebrate and understand Christ's humanity and divinity, it became a central tenet of the Christian faith that salvation was grounded in the Son of God taking on human flesh in the person of Jesus Christ. The term in-carnation can be translated as in-fleshing. Thus, at Christmas we celebrate Immanuel—God is with us! Salvation is that God became fully human in every way we are. Hence, as God becomes flesh, this uniting of humanity and divinity heals and redeems sinful diseased humanity.

Not only should Bethlehem also be counted as central to the gospel story, the church has recorded Jesus' teachings and miracles to be a means of life and transformation for the church. If the church did not feel Jesus' life and teachings were significant they would not have included them in the Scriptures. Moreover, it is safe to say it is Jesus' life and teachings that saw Him as a threat to the Jewish and Roman leaders. While the Romans saw Jesus largely as a nuisance, the Jewish leaders saw Him as a direct threat to the faith. As one celebrates the death and resurrection of Jesus, all of His birth, life, teachings and ministry must be connected as central to the salvation story.

Where is the Hope?

I love the church and I love Christians. However, as a pastor and theologian one of my primary places of sadness for Christians is their leaning towards fear and despair. While the reasons for this are numerous, it is striking that for a people of faith in the life, death, resurrection, and coming again in glory of Jesus, there is so much despair and fear choking out the life of Christians. The parable of the sower in Matthew 13:22 teaches that the seed that falls among thorns dies because of the worries of life and the deceitfulness of wealth choke all joy and life from it. I have known too many Christians oppressed by fear and despair. Conversely, the culmination of Christ's life in the death and resurrection are to be the foundation of hope. We believe that God's kingdom is coming to earth more every day. We hope in God's love being more fully embodied all over the world. Moreover, within God's kingdom coming we are also starkly aware of the practices, people, and institutions who are not living into God's kingdom of redeeming love.

Here becomes the main thrust. The life, death, and resurrection of Jesus is not focused on transporting our disembodied soul to heaven. While each person matters desperately to God, each person's healing is part of God's larger work of redeeming all of creation.

To fully live into the hope and healing of the death and resurrection of Jesus, we are not to be observers, but followers. Through baptism, we put to death the way of sin so that we can be raised with Christ into a life of joy and freedom (Romans 6:1-6). This life of love invites us to then be sent by God to participate in the world's redemption as part of our ongoing discipleship. We are not called to observe Christ's death and resurrection, we are called to pick up our cross and follow Christ in a ministry of compassion, love, and hospitality (Matthew 16:24-26). We work out our salvation by allowing the Spirit to participate in God's love and healing to those who are godless and without hope and those who are godforsaken and God has not stopped pain and tragedy from visiting their home. Let us live and minister in the hope of Christ's death and resurrection.

---

*See *Crucified God* (Minneapolis: Fortress Press, 1993).

BRENT PETERSON is an ordained elder in the Church of the Nazarene. He is currently the Dean of the College of Theology and Christian Ministries at Northwest Nazarene University and also serves as Pastor of Spiritual and Liturgical Formation at College Church of the Nazarene in Nampa, Idaho.

SESSION 1

Session Outcome

To help people understand the relationship between Jesus' sacrifice and the Passover, and celebrate their participation in the new covenant.

Customize:

Spirit is the password to access expanded teaching helps on FoundryLeader.com.

Discover:

Illustrated Bible Life fills in a little background about Mark the gospel writer, and provides verse-by-verse commentary on the Scripture passage.

Four World-Changing Days

March

5

CELEBRATING PASSOVER

Jesus instituted the Lord's Supper as the symbol of a new covenant God was making with humanity.

THE WORD

MARK 14:12-26

On the first day of the Festival of Unleavened Bread, when it was customary to sacrifice the Passover lamb, Jesus' disciples asked him, "Where do you want us to go and make preparations for you to eat the Passover?"

¹³So he sent two of his disciples, telling them, "Go into the city, and a man carrying a jar of water will meet you. Follow him. ¹⁴Say to the owner of the house he enters, 'The Teacher asks: Where is my guest room, where I may eat the Passover with my disciples?' ¹⁵He will show you a large room upstairs, furnished and ready. Make preparations for us there."

¹⁶The disciples left, went into the city and found things just as Jesus had told them. So they prepared the Passover.

¹⁷When evening came, Jesus arrived with the Twelve. ¹⁸While they were reclining at the table eating, he said, "Truly I tell you, one of you will betray me—one who is eating with me."

¹⁹They were saddened, and one by one they said to him, "Surely you don't mean me?"

²⁰"It is one of the Twelve," he replied, "one who dips bread into the bowl with me. ²¹The Son of Man will go just as it is written about him. But woe to that man who betrays the Son of Man! It would be better for him if he had not been born."

²²While they were eating, Jesus took bread, and when he had given thanks, he broke it and gave it to his disciples, saying, "Take it; this is my body."

²³Then he took a cup, and when he had given thanks, he gave it to them, and they all drank from it.

Last Week:

We saw the rippling results of sin.

This Week:

We will see the meaning and message of the Lord's Supper.

Session 1

KEY VERSE ²⁴**"This is my blood of the covenant, which is poured out for many," he said to them.** ²⁵"Truly I tell you, I will not drink again from the fruit of the vine until that day when I drink it new in the kingdom of God."

²⁶When they had sung a hymn, they went out to the Mount of Olives.

ENGAGE THE WORD

PREPARATION FOR PASSOVER

Mark 14:12-16

The passage begins with Mark's reference to the Festival of Unleavened Bread and the custom of sacrificing the Passover lamb. This was not only a historical marker of time, but also a literary foreshadowing of the impending death of Jesus.

The disciples seemed to be worried about the necessity of preparing for the Passover celebration. Taking the initiative, they asked Jesus about the necessary preparations. If they were anxious about the preparations, they did not need to be. As always in Mark's gospel, Jesus was ready, prepared, and in control.

After the triumphal entry and Jesus' clearing of the temple (Mark 11:1-19), the conflict between Jesus and the Jewish religious leaders had reached a boiling point. Previously, Mark pointed out the chief priests and teachers of the law were conspiring a way to kill Jesus (Mark 11:18). As a result, Jesus' instructions for the preparation of the Passover reflected careful and thoughtful planning. Jesus sent two of His disciples to Jerusalem with instructions resembling coded messages and secret arrangements. Arriving in the city, they found things just as Jesus had told them, and they prepared the Passover as He had commanded.

PREDICTION OF BETRAYAL

Mark 14:17-21

In the evening of the Passover, Jesus shared the Passover meal with His disciples. The sharing of food had more significance for Jews than merely a social gathering. Covenants were typically sealed with a

▶ **Watch:**

Dr. Roger Hahn introduces this unit on "Four World-Changing Days."

🔊 **Listen:**

FoundryLeader.com: This week's *Illustrated Bible Life* "Article Out Loud" delves into what we know about the writer of the Gospel of Mark.

Notes:

_____

_____

_____

_____

_____

_____

_____

_____

_____

_____

_____

_____

_____

_____

_____

_____

_____

_____

Did You Know?
The Lord's Supper is traditionally referred to as the "Eucharist," which is derived from Mark 14:23 where Jesus "gave thanks" (Greek: *eucharistēsas*) before He passed around the cup.

meal (for instance, Abimelech and Isaac, Genesis 26:26-31; Laban and Jacob, Genesis 31:51-54). During the meal, Jesus made a shocking announcement: "One of you is going to betray me" (v. 18). To betray the one who had shared his bread was a grievous offence, and the disciples were saddened and alarmed.

The incredible shock of the disciples was reflected in their individual responses to Jesus as they each asked, "Surely you don't mean me?" Mark did not specifically identify Judas in this passage as the offender. However, his notation that the disciples asked this question "one by one" revealed the blatant and deceptive lies of Judas who faked his own innocence even while planning the details of the betrayal.

Jesus confirmed that His betrayer was one of the Twelve who "dips bread into the bowl with me." This phrase is an allusion to Psalm 41:9 and the righteous sufferer, whom the psalmist confidently assured that God would vindicate and exalt (41:10-13). Jesus' words in verse 21 explicitly connected the Son of Man (Jesus' favorite self-designation) with the one who suffers unjustly for righteousness. The concept of a "suffering Messiah" did not match any of the Jewish expectations, and yet Jesus affirmed that His suffering was foretold in Scripture. Although the events of Jesus' passion that were soon to unfold would be painful and horrifying, Jesus reassured His disciples that His betrayal would not impede God's plan, but would actually be used to accomplish God's salvational purposes. Nonetheless, the betrayer was fully responsible and culpable for his willing participation in this hideous double-cross.

THE LORD'S SUPPER   Mark 14:22-26

In the Passover meal, bread is broken and wine is consumed as essential parts of the Jewish people's celebration of God's deliverance of them from Egypt and His covenant with them as His favored people. At Jesus' Passover celebration with His disciples, He explicitly connected the elements of this meal to His

Discover:

About 30 years after the death and resurrection of Jesus, few disciples who had walked with Jesus were still alive. So, a man named Mark wrote the first biography of Jesus. Who was Mark? Let's find out in this week's *Illustrated Bible Life* article, "Mark, the First Biographer of Jesus."

Think About It

John referred specifically to at least three different Passovers Jesus celebrated in Jerusalem. By contrast, Matthew, Mark, and Luke only mention the one Passover when Jesus was arrested, tried, crucified, and resurrected.

imminent suffering and death, as well as to the new covenant He was establishing with them.

At some time during the supper, Jesus took bread, gave thanks, broke it, and gave it to His disciples. It is interesting to note these very same verbs—took, gave thanks, broke, and gave (to His disciples)—were used in the miraculous feeding of the 5,000 (Mark 6:41) and the 4,000 (Mark 8:6). Here, though, Jesus identified the bread with the words, "This is my body." Jesus identified himself in a profound way with the broken bread, and He invited His followers to join Him in eating the bread.

He also took the cup, gave thanks, gave it to His disciples, and they all drank from the one cup. Mark's language emphasized the intimate and significant participation of the disciples in Jesus' actions of eating and drinking. Jesus explained, "This is my blood of the covenant, which is poured out for many." We cannot overlook the fact Jesus uttered these words during a Passover meal that commemorated Israel's deliverance from bondage and God's covenant with the Jewish people. Now, on the eve of His horrific death and glorious resurrection, Jesus used these elements to forever mark His coming death and resurrection as a deliverance from sin and death, as well as the establishment of a new covenant of God's grace and favor on all who believe and follow Jesus. The supper that began on such a sad note ended with a note of glorious victory as Jesus anticipated the celebration of the coming kingdom of God after His resurrection.

REFLECT Take time to consider the way Jesus established a new covenant of God's grace and favor on all who believe.

DANIEL G. POWERS is co-director of the Bible and Theology program and professor of New Testament at Nazarene Bible College.

Notes:

_____
_____
_____
_____
_____
_____
_____
_____
_____
_____
_____
_____
_____
_____
_____
_____
_____

Discussion Guide

 Connect to My Experience

I love eating. Even more, I love eating with other people. Growing up as the youngest of five children, it seems I've always been eating with company present. Those meals were formative. Something special took place around our dining table.

- Were you raised in a home that gathered around the table for family meals? What was your practice?

- How did that table time shape you?

- Do you have any memorable meals that stand out? Share your experience with the group.

Transition:

In today's text, we encounter a meal unlike any other. This meal radically shaped those present and continues to shape us today.

 **Connect to the Word**

Invite someone to read Mark 14:12-16, then discuss the following,

Mark immediately connects the Last Supper with the events of the Festival of Unleavened Bread and with the Passover meal.

- What is the significance of the fact that this passage takes place during the Passover? (The Passover commemorates the time when the angel of the Lord "passed over" the homes of the Hebrews rather than killing the firstborn sons, as happened in the Egyptian homes. The sign that the angel should pass over these homes was the blood of a lamb spread on the doorframes of the house.)

- Why is it significant for Mark to link Jesus' story with the events of the Passover? What continuity do we see in God's story?

The disciples were seeking directions from Jesus for preparation of the Passover meal.

- What are the ways we prepare our hearts to experience the presence of God in our lives?

- How do you think the disciples felt when they "found things just as Jesus had told them"? (v.16) What would have been going through your mind?

Invite someone to read Mark 14:17-21, then discuss the following,

During the meal Jesus announced that one would betray Him.

- When you think of Jesus sharing a meal with friends, what do you think the mood would be as they gathered? How do Jesus' first recorded words at this Passover meal change the tone or mood?

- Read Psalm 41:9-12. How does this psalm speak to the events that will follow for Jesus?

- Mark records that each of the disciples, "one by one," asked Jesus, "Surely, you don't mean me?" (v.19) Why does Mark note that each person asked that question in succession?

- Instead of Jesus saying, "It is one of you," why does Jesus say, "It is one of the Twelve" (v. 20)? (Possibly to note the close relationship that Jesus had with these disciples.)

- If Jesus is sure that His betrayer reclines at the table and shares this meal with Him, why does Jesus go through with this meal? Why do you think Jesus

Insight

When the ancient Jews participated in the Passover meal, their minds turned to one thing—the grace and mercy of God that had saved their lives in Egypt. When Christians today read the passage about the Lord's Supper, our minds should turn to one thing—the grace and mercy of God, as manifested in the body and blood of Jesus, that has saved our lives from sin.

Invite someone to read Mark 14:22-26, then discuss the following,

didn't keep Judas out of this gathering? Does this tell us anything about the nature of God? If so, what?

The disciples were given the opportunity to examine their hearts to see who was the one who would prove unfaithful.

- In what ways can we take advantage of opportunities to examine our journey with Jesus?

Bread and wine would have been consumed as part of the Passover meal.

- How does Jesus interpret these elements? (He identifies them with His body and blood.)
- In what ways is Jesus the Passover Lamb? (Faith in Jesus brings spiritual deliverance, just as God used the shed blood of the Passover lamb to bring the Hebrews deliverance from Egypt.)

Jesus shares the bread and cup—His body and blood—with all present, including Judas. He also says that His blood is "poured out for many" (v. 24).

- How is the inclusiveness of this new covenant different from the old covenant? (This sacrificial Lamb, Jesus, would be a once and for all, totally sufficient sacrifice for sin. His cleansing blood would extend to all people for all generations.)
- In verse 25, what sign of hope does Jesus provide?

Connect to My Life and the World

Bring your session to a close by asking the following,

- Jesus sent the disciples out at the beginning of the story. Would you trust Jesus to send you on a mission if you weren't certain how things would play out? If so, how does that trust get built?

Participating in the Lord's Supper shapes and forms our identity.

- How does the continued celebration of the Lord's Supper shape us? (We are reminded that Jesus is the host, not us; God brings life out of death; We are people of the cross; We entrust ourselves to God's future; We are dependent upon God's provisions.)
- Do you ever find yourself wanting to draw boundaries around the table, thus determining who can participate and who cannot? Why do we tend to do that?
- What does it mean to you that Jesus invited Judas to the table and continued to dine with him even after Judas tried to hide his betrayal?
- When we read this passage in light of the exodus event, what is the new exodus that Jesus provides? What are we saved from, and what are we saved for?

As you close, thank God for the life and salvation that Jesus offers.

Sessions 1-6 are written by Jon Gildner

Jon currently serves as the Executive Pastor of Discipleship and Administration at Central Church of the Nazarene in Flint, MI.

Unit 1

Four World-Changing Days

March

12

PREPARING FOR THE CROSS

Jesus' prayer in the Garden of Gethsemane is an example of surrender to God's will for all believers to follow.

THE WORD

MARK 14:32-50

They went to a place called Gethsemane, and Jesus said to his disciples, "Sit here while I pray." ³³He took Peter, James and John along with him, and he began to be deeply distressed and troubled. ³⁴"My soul is overwhelmed with sorrow to the point of death," he said to them. "Stay here and keep watch."

³⁵Going a little farther, he fell to the ground and prayed that if possible the hour might pass from him. **³⁶"Abba, Father," he said,**

KEY VERSE

"everything is possible for you. Take this cup from me. Yet not what I will, but what you will."

³⁷Then he returned to his disciples and found them sleeping. "Simon," he said to Peter, "are you asleep? Couldn't you keep watch for one hour? ³⁸Watch and pray so that you will not fall into temptation. The spirit is willing, but the flesh is weak."

³⁹Once more he went away and prayed the same thing. ⁴⁰When he came back, he again found them sleeping, because their eyes were heavy. They did not know what to say to him.

⁴¹Returning the third time, he said to them, "Are you still sleeping and resting? Enough! The hour has come. Look, the Son of Man is delivered into the hands of sinners. ⁴²Rise! Let us go! Here comes my betrayer!"

⁴³Just as he was speaking, Judas, one of the Twelve, appeared. With him was a crowd armed with swords and clubs, sent from the chief priests, the teachers of the law, and the elders.

⁴⁴Now the betrayer had arranged a signal with them: "The one I kiss is the man; arrest him and lead him away under guard." ⁴⁵Going at once to Jesus, Judas said, "Rabbi!" and kissed him. ⁴⁶The men

Last Week:

We discovered how the Lord's Supper is a celebration of the new covenant.

This Week:

We will discover that prayer had a significant place in the spiritual life of Jesus.

_____

_____

_____

_____

_____

_____

_____

_____

_____

_____

_____

_____

_____

_____

_____

_____

_____

_____

_____

Session 2

seized Jesus and arrested him. ⁴⁷Then one of those standing near drew his sword and struck the servant of the high priest, cutting off his ear.

⁴⁸"Am I leading a rebellion," said Jesus, "that you have come out with swords and clubs to capture me? ⁴⁹Every day I was with you, teaching in the temple courts, and you did not arrest me. But the Scripture must be fulfilled." ⁵⁰Then everyone deserted him and fled.

ENGAGE THE WORD

PRAYER AND SURRENDER

Mark 14:32-36

Leaving the upper room where they had celebrated the Passover meal together, Jesus took His disciples to Gethsemane in order to pray. On two other occasions in Mark's gospel, Jesus had selected Peter, James, and John to accompany Him during a special moment. This "inner group of three disciples" was given the opportunity to witness Jesus' life-giving power when He raised Jairus' daughter back to life (5:37-43), and they also watched in wonder as Jesus was transformed in glory on the Mount of Transfiguration (9:2-9). Now Jesus brought them along to watch and support Him as He agonized in prayer during the longest and most difficult night of His life. Jesus' victory over sin and death would be won through His resurrection; His victory over anxiety and fear were won in Gethsemane that night through His prayers.

Mark candidly displayed Jesus' anxiety and distress. Jesus told His three companions that He was grieved with sorrow to the point of death. Jesus' humanity is on full display in these anxious moments as He faced the pain and fear of impending torture and death. But as the beloved Son of God, Jesus also carried the heavy burden of experiencing disjunction from His Father as He would bear the sins of the world. Thus, in the fullness of both His humanity and divinity, Jesus experienced the overwhelming significance and depth of the trial He faced.

Asking His friends to keep watch with Him in prayer, Jesus went a little further, fell to the ground,

🔊 **Listen:**

FoundryLeader.com: What does it mean that Jesus had both a human nature and a divine one, and why is this important? This week's *Illustrated Bible Life* "Article Out Loud" explains.

Notes:

_____

_____

_____

_____

_____

_____

_____

_____

_____

_____

_____

_____

_____

_____

_____

_____

_____

Did You Know?
Matthew, Mark, and Luke referred to the place where Jesus agonized in prayer as "Gethsemane." Only John's gospel referred to Gethsemane as the "Garden" of Gethsemane.

and prayed that God would spare Him from this hour. The very personal title "Abba, Father" revealed the intimacy of this prayer. This was not a prayer of disobedience. Since "everything is possible" for God, Jesus knew that God had the power to take the cup of suffering and death away from Him. But most importantly, Jesus wanted God's will to be done. In this honest prayer, in the moment of His deepest anxiety and fear, Jesus sharply distinguished between His will and the will of the Father. And in prayer, He resigned himself to the accomplishment of the Father's will, regardless of the decision's painful consequences. Jesus modeled for all time that the essence of being a Christian is to face difficult situations while choosing to do God's will.

WILLING SPIRIT, WEAK FLESH

Mark 14:37-42

When Jesus came back to the disciples, He found them sleeping. To Peter, who just moments before had declared that he would never fall away, Jesus asked, "Could you not watch and pray for just one hour?" The key to overcoming times of "weak flesh" is not found in boastful claims or confident expressions of faith, but in watchful prayer.

Jesus left the disciples two more times in Gethsemane to pray and align His will with the will of the Father. Each time He returned to find His three trusted companions sleeping instead of praying. The third time He declared, "Enough! The hour has come."

Then Jesus said to them, "Rise! Let us go!" These words demonstrated that He had prayed through to victory and the acceptance of God's will. As His betrayer drew near, Jesus would not try to escape His captors or to fight back with violence. His will was conformed to God's will.

BETRAYAL AND ARREST OF JESUS

Mark 14:43-50

Whereas the previous verses depicted Jesus' struggle and victory over anxiety and fear through prayer,

Discover:

When Jesus prayed in the Garden of Gethsemane for God to take the cup of suffering that was set before Him that night, this obviously human act raised a question for many of us. Wasn't Jesus God? Why would He pray such a prayer? This week's *Illustrated Bible Life* article, "Fully Human, Fully Divine," explores this complex theological issue.

_____

_____

_____

_____

_____

_____

Session 2

Think About It

"Cup" can refer to suffering and death (Mark 10:38), but it can also refer to God's wrathful judgment on sin (Isaiah 51:17). By drinking the "cup," Jesus innocently experienced both death and the judgmental penalty for the sins of others.

Mark now described the pathetic performance of Jesus' disciples in this crucial moment of arrest. First, the leader of the arresting mob is Judas, whom Mark explicitly identified as one of the 12 disciples. Just as Jesus foretold, one of His very own chosen disciples betrayed Him. With painful irony, Judas addressed Jesus with the title "Rabbi," which was an esteemed name for a respected teacher. Furthermore, Judas greeted Jesus with a kiss, which was often a sign of warm affection between a disciple and his teacher. With brazen hypocrisy, Judas denigrated these gestures of love and respect into signs of betrayal and death.

When the arresting mob seized and arrested Jesus, one of Jesus' followers drew his sword and sliced off the ear of the high priest's servant. Although Mark did not identify the offender, John's gospel identified him as Peter.

Jesus quickly stopped the fighting. He rebuked the cowardly timing of His accusers, who were too frightened of the crowds to arrest Jesus while He was teaching openly in the temple courts. Instead, the religious leaders sent a violent and armed mob in the dead of night to do their dirty work.

Jesus' earlier prediction to the disciples that "you will all fall away" (14:27) was then fulfilled. All Jesus' disciples abandoned Him and ran away. But Jesus did not resist. With calm submission to God, Jesus surrendered himself to His captors, thereby setting into motion the fulfillment of Scripture's promise of God's salvation for all who believe.

_____

_____

_____

_____

_____

_____

REFLECT If you are experiencing a "weakened flesh" in an area of your life, take it to God in prayer.

DANIEL G. POWERS

_____

_____

Discussion Guide

Connect to My Experience

One of the areas of the Christian life many people feel they should do more of and should be better at is prayer. As believers, we may feel guilt over our prayer life, or lack of a prayer life.

- What is prayer? How would you define it?
- How would you describe your experience with prayer in your faith journey?
- Have you ever experienced feelings of guilt over your prayer life? If so, in what way?
- Have you discovered that your prayer life has changed over time? What patterns have you noticed over the years?

Transition:

In today's passage, we find Jesus and a few disciples struggling with prayer, albeit for different reasons.

Connect to the Word

Invite someone to read Mark 14:32-36, then discuss the following,

Jesus chose to spend the closing hours of His life on earth in communion with His friends and in prayer with His Father. The setting was Gethsemane, one of the many private, walled gardens outside the city of Jerusalem.

- What does the writer tell us about how Jesus is feeling? How does Jesus himself describe His current state?

Mark doesn't hide the fact that Jesus, the Son of God, the Messiah, is in anguish. He even brought some friends to keep Him company.

- What else does Mark tell us that reveals Jesus' emotional state? What does this display of emotion and vulnerability tell us about Jesus?

Mark says that Jesus left Peter, James, and John to keep watch. Then he adds, "Going a little farther, he fell to the ground" (v.35).

- Since Jews normally stood to pray with their hands lifted toward heaven (Matthew 6:5; Luke 18:11, 13; 1 Timothy 2:8), what did it mean for Jesus to "fall" to the ground (v. 32)?
- What do you think Jesus meant when He prayed, "Everything is possible for you. Take this cup from me"?
- How does Jesus' prayer in verse 36 shape your understanding and approach to prayer? Based on this verse alone, how would you define prayer?

Invite someone to read Mark 14:37-42, then discuss the following,

When Jesus returned and found the disciples sleeping, He addressed Peter specifically saying, "Simon."

- What do you think is the temptation to which Jesus refers (v. 38)? (The temptation is to deny Jesus and fall away, it's not about falling asleep.)
- How does watchfulness and prayer help thwart temptation?
- How would you interpret Jesus' words, "The spirit is willing, but the body is weak"?

Jesus finds His closest friends sleeping each time He returns from prayer.

- Do you think Jesus was frustrated with them simply because they were tired and dozed off, or is there something more happening here? What might their inability to stay awake reveal about their awareness of the ensuing events?

Insight

This account shows us the darkest night Jesus experienced on this earth. This account shows us that the Christian life is not always easy. Sometimes the path goes through dark situations. Jesus was as close to the Father as a person ever gets, yet He experienced Gethsemane. However, He did not go through it alone. The Father was near Him and strengthened Him.

Invite someone to read Mark 14:43-50, then discuss the following,

■ Why do you think the disciples did not have the same kind of urgency demonstrated by Jesus?

Judas led an armed group to the secluded garden where Jesus was praying. He identified Jesus as the one to seize and restrain by greeting Him with a kiss.

■ Since Judas knew Jesus to be a peace-loving teacher, why do you think he thought there might be a need for an armed detachment of soldiers to arrest Him?

Judas addresses Jesus as "Rabbi." Jesus has been Judas' teacher. Jesus has taken him in, walked with him, and given him glimpses of the kingdom.

■ How do you account for Judas' betrayal? Did he fail to learn something that Jesus taught, or is there more to it? Explain.

Although Mark hides the identity of the one who cut off the ear of the servant of the high priest, John's gospel tells us it was Peter.

■ Could Peter's actions here be connected to his lack of prayer and watchfulness in the garden? Did he fail to grasp the nature of Jesus' kingdom? Why or why not?

This account ends with everyone deserting Jesus.

■ How does this story affect your understanding of what prayer is and what it seeks to accomplish?

Connect to My Life and the World

Jesus found the strength to surrender to the will of God and submit to the suffering of the cross in the place of prayer.

■ As you've engaged with this session today, what stands out to you most about Jesus' time in prayer?

■ How does this account of Jesus in the garden establish a new paradigm for prayer?

Jesus didn't get what He prayed for. The rescue didn't come in the way He had prayed.

■ How do you respond when God doesn't show up in the way you want?

■ Is there a specific prayer that keeps you going back to God? What are you waiting on God for? In light of today's session, are you sensing God saying anything new to you?

Sometimes obedience to the will of God leads to the loss of personal relationships.

■ Have you ever experienced this? How have you experienced God's faithfulness in the midst of loneliness?

Jesus the Messiah experienced pain, betrayal, and loneliness.

■ Does it bring you comfort knowing that Jesus experienced the same lows you experience? If so, in what ways?

■ Do you think there was "victory" achieved in the garden? Why or why not? What does victory in prayer look like?

As you close this session, ask God to conform your will to God's will.

Unit 1

Four World-Changing Days

Session Outcome

To help people acknowledge the reality of failure and offer hope that failure need not be final.

Customize:

Spirit is the password to access expanded teaching helps on FoundryLeader.com.

Discover:

Where did Jesus spend His last hours on earth? *Illustrated Bible Life* takes a look at one of these sites, and provides verse-by-verse commentary on the Scripture passage.

March

19

TRAGIC FAILURE OF LOYALTY

When failure happens, it need not be final.

THE WORD

MARK 14:27-31

"You will all fall away," Jesus told them, "for it is written: "'I will strike the shepherd, and the sheep will be scattered.'

²⁸But after I have risen, I will go ahead of you into Galilee."

²⁹Peter declared, "Even if all fall away, I will not."

³⁰"Truly I tell you," Jesus answered, "today—yes, tonight—before the rooster crows twice you yourself will disown me three times."

³¹But Peter insisted emphatically, "Even if I have to die with you, I will never disown you." And all the others said the same.

66-72

⁶⁶While Peter was below in the courtyard, one of the servant girls of the high priest came by. ⁶⁷When she saw Peter warming himself, she looked closely at him.

"You also were with that Nazarene, Jesus," she said.

⁶⁸But he denied it. "I don't know or understand what you're talking about," he said, and went out into the entryway.

⁶⁹When the servant girl saw him there, she said again to those standing around, "This fellow is one of them." ⁷⁰Again he denied it.

After a little while, those standing near said to Peter, "Surely you are one of them, for you are a Galilean."

⁷¹He began to call down curses, and he swore to them, "I don't know this man you're talking about."

KEY VERSE ⁷²**Immediately the rooster crowed the second time. Then Peter remembered the word Jesus had spoken to him: "Before the rooster crows twice you will disown me three times." And he broke down and wept.**

Last Week:

We learned that believers must come to a place of submission and surrender to God's will.

This Week:

We will learn that God is always ready to restore those who have fallen.

Session 3

ENGAGE THE WORD

PREDICTIONS OF ABANDONMENT AND DISOWNING

Mark 14:27-31

After the Last Supper, Jesus led His disciples toward Gethsemane. The disciples were undoubtedly shaken up by Jesus' earlier announcement that one of them would betray Him. Now Jesus jolted them by predicting that they would all abandon Him and fall away. Quoting Zechariah 13:7, Jesus declared that the disciples would scatter and forsake Him just as sheep scatter when their shepherd is struck down.

With indignant self-righteousness, Peter confidently proclaimed that, even if all the rest of Jesus' followers would fall away, he would stand loyal and faithful to Jesus. Peter's impetuous pride came into full view in this moment. Apparently, Peter had no difficulty in accepting the Lord's word that the other disciples would fall away, but he vehemently denied any possibility of his own failure or disloyalty to Jesus. Unfortunately, bold affirmations of fidelity are no guarantee for faithfulness. The disheartening lesson for today is that anyone can stumble and fall on the path of following Christ. The good news is that failure does not need to be final.

Jesus knew that Peter would deny Him. Indeed, Jesus told Peter he would disown Jesus three times before the rooster crowed twice in the early morning. Peter emphatically refused to accept what Jesus said to him. He insisted that, even if it meant his own death, he would never disown Jesus. Mark added that all the other disciples joined Peter in saying the same thing.

In the midst of this shocking announcement of the failure and abandonment of the disciples and Peter, the reassuring promise and hope of verse 28 was probably overlooked by most of the disciples. Despite the failure and abandonment of the disciples, and despite the impending arrest, suffering, and even death of Jesus, this would not be the last word. Jesus promised His disciples that after He had risen, He would go ahead of them into Galilee. The reality of failure can often seem to destroy and darken every prospect of

🔊 **Listen:**

FoundryLeader.com: This week's *Illustrated Bible Life* "Article Out Loud" explores the Church of St. Peter in Gallicantu in Jerusalem, possible site of Jesus' trial before the high priest and of Peter's denial of Jesus.

Notes:

_____

_____

_____

_____

_____

_____

_____

_____

_____

_____

_____

_____

_____

_____

_____

_____

_____

Did You Know?
Early Christian tradition claims that Mark's main source for his gospel was Simon Peter himself. If this is true, Mark's story of Peter's denial is actually Peter's own story.

PETER'S THREEFOLD DENIAL

hope or restoration. Even though the disciples certainly did not understand Him in that moment, Jesus did not only foretell their failure, but He also foretold His ultimate victory: Jesus would arise and gather them to himself again.

Mark 14:66-72

Despite Peter's adamant reassurance and pledge of loyalty, the fulfillment of Jesus' solemn prediction of His denial did not take long to unfold. Mark carefully portrayed Peter's denials as taking place simultaneously with Jesus' trial before the Jewish ruling council. While Jesus was being accused and challenged by the powerful high priest and the council, Peter was accused and challenged by the priest's powerless female servant. Likewise, while Jesus stood firm and fast under the penetrating scrutiny of the blood-thirsty Jewish authorities, Peter crumbled and collapsed under the slightest weight of pressure and accusation. The contrasts Mark portrayed between Jesus and Peter were vivid and deliberate.

To Peter's credit, the narrative of his denial began in the courtyard near the location of Jesus' trial. Even though the other disciples had run away, Peter continued to follow Jesus, albeit at a distance. In rapid succession, however, Peter disclaimed and denied any knowledge or relationship with Jesus three times. Notably, the denials grew more adamant and emphatic each time Peter was confronted.

The priest's slave girl issued the first two challenges. Looking closely at Peter's face, she accused Peter derisively of association with "that Nazarene Jesus." Peter strongly denied any knowledge or understanding of what she said, and he quickly moved away from the light of the fire into the entryway. Seeing Peter a little later in the entryway, the girl repeated her accusation against Peter to those who were standing close by. Peter again denied any association with Jesus.

Shortly thereafter, the tensions escalated as now

 **Discover:**

A stone's throw away from the Old City of Jerusalem, the Church of St. Peter in Gallicantu stands on the eastern slopes of Mount Zion. The name of the church evokes one of the most gripping scenes in the gospels. "Gallicantu" comes from the Latin expression, galli cantu, "The rooster crows," reminiscent of Peter's triple denial of Jesus. This week's *Illustrated Bible Life* article, "The Church of St. Peter in Gallicantu," takes a look at this ancient site.

Notes:

_____

_____

_____

_____

_____

_____

_____

_____

_____

_____

_____

_____

_____

_____

_____

_____

_____

_____

Session 3

Think About It

Peter's threefold denial corresponds with his threefold failure to watch and pray with Jesus in Gethsemane (Mark 14:34-41). Victory over temptation is often gained beforehand in our persistent prayer life.

the other bystanders in the courtyard began to accuse Peter of affiliation with Jesus, since Peter was also from the region of Galilee. Undoubtedly, Peter's Galilean accent betrayed his birthplace and background to his accusers. Peter's third denial in verse 71 is as vehement as his pledge of loyalty was in verse 31. With loud and heated curses, Peter swore that he did not know Jesus.

The verb "call down curses" in verse 71 does not have an object in the Greek text. It can be translated in two different ways. It may mean that Peter denied Jesus under oath and called down curses on himself if he was lying, or it may mean that Peter actually pronounced a curse on Jesus. In later years, when Christians faced official persecution from the Romans, cursing Christ was considered proof positive that a person was not a Christian. Regardless of the translation, the failure and fall of Peter were abysmal and complete.

No sooner were the words of denial and solemn curses out of Peter's mouth than the rooster crowed the second time. Jesus' prophetic words were proven true to the very letter. When Peter recognized the magnitude of his failure, he broke down and wept bitterly. Self-awareness and brokenness are often the beginning of growth and restoration.

Even though the passage for this week ends at this tragic place, by the grace of God the story was not over. Jesus was prepared to deal with the damage of displaced loyalty and even blatant denial because His love knew no limits. Our best intentions and faithfulness to Christ may sometimes waver and even fail, but our failure does not need to be final. We have the blessed assurance that the love and grace of Jesus never fail!

REFLECT Take time to thank God for His mercy and grace.

DANIEL G. POWERS

Discussion Guide

Connect to My Experience

There is an old saying that goes like this: "If at first you don't succeed, try and try again." However, many of us give up when we do not succeed the first time. No one likes to fail.

- Why is failure so painful?
- Why do we tend to remember our failures more than our successes?
- In what ways can a failure keep us from succeeding in other areas of our life?
- How do you deal with and overcome failure in your life?

Transition:

In today's session we encounter the failure of Peter, as well as the faithful love of Jesus.

Connect to the Word

Invite someone to read Mark 14:27-31, then discuss the following,

In verse 18, Jesus shocked His disciples when He told them that one of them would betray Him. One of the inner-circle would fail to carry out the way of living Jesus had been teaching them. In verse 27, Jesus tells the group that all of them will "fall away."

- How do you think the disciples might have felt after that supper together?
- If Jesus had told you that you would fall away, how would you have reacted?
- Why do sheep scatter when the shepherd goes down? From what we know, how does this apply to Jesus and the disciples?
- In verse 28, what are the promises that Jesus gives to the flailing disciples? (He will rise again after His death. He will go ahead of them.)
- In saying that He will go ahead of them into Galilee, what is Jesus conveying to His disciples? (They will join Him there. Their failure won't mark the end of their relationship with Him.)

Even though Jesus says that "all" will fall away, Peter declares he would not.

- What does this communicate about Peter? (feels he knows more about himself than Jesus does; he wants to do the right thing)
- Most likely Peter said this in front of the others, so how do you think the other disciples felt about Peter's statement? How can our own pride or lack of self-awareness impact our relationship with God and others?
- What can we learn from Peter's brash insistence of his faithfulness? (1] Listen to what the Lord has to say to us. 2] Saying we will be faithful is not as important as being faithful.)

Verse 31 also says, "All the others said the same." Their eyes and ears were seemingly fixed on Peter, not the Master.

- What can we learn from their response? (We must listen carefully to what the Lord has to say and keep our eyes fixed on Him.)

Invite someone to read Mark 14:66-72, then discuss the following,

In verse 50 we are told that everyone deserted Jesus; however, we later learn that Peter followed Jesus at a distance, "right into the courtyard of the high priest" (v. 54).

- What does this tell us about Peter? Do you see his behavior in a positive or negative light? Why?
- What does Mark tell us about the identity and role of Peter's first accuser?

Insight

If we fail, Christ wants to restore us (1 John 2:1). Our Lord always seeks to bring us back. But for that to take place, we must fall broken before Him and admit our need. When we are humble and contrite, we can be sure He will restore us. Peter failed Jesus. However, Jesus did not allow the story to end there. Jesus found a way of restoration. He does the same today!

■ Would this person have had much status in that culture? How does this compare to Jesus' accusers? (see vv. 53, 55)

In verse 61, Jesus is asked about His identity and He tells the high priest that He is the Messiah, the Son of the Blessed One. While Jesus was on trial, Peter was being tried before a servant girl.

■ What is Peter's reply when he is asked about His connection to Jesus (v. 68)?

■ What is the contrast between Jesus and Peter in this incident? (Jesus is an example of what we should emulate; Peter of what we should avoid. Jesus is an example of courage; Peter an example of cowardice. Jesus is a faithful witness; Peter an unfaithful one.)

Peter says, "I don't know this man you're talking about."

■ In what way is Peter telling the truth?

■ How does Peter's acknowledgement reveal that he didn't know or understand who Jesus was?

Mark says that it wasn't until the rooster crowed the second time that Peter remembered what Jesus had said about this coming to pass.

■ What could have kept Peter from realizing this sooner? How could he not see himself disowning Jesus in his earlier denials to the servant girl? (self-preservation; saving himself took precedent)

■ Why do you think Peter breaks down and weeps?

■ Jesus used a rooster to remind Peter of his weakness. What reminds us of our daily need of God's help?

Connect to My Life and the World

Peter and the other disciples had their fidelity to Jesus tested in ways they had never experienced before.

■ What situations have you faced that have tested your fidelity to Jesus? How did you get through those times?

■ Presumably there are sisters and brothers in the faith going through tremendous trials. How can the church help those who are wavering?

■ When you think about Peter's actions in this story, at what point do you most connect with him?

■ Verse 28 says, "But after I have risen, I will go ahead of you into Galilee." What does this verse reveal about the limits of spiritual/physical death and failure? (Jesus has victory over sin and death and goes ahead of us.)

Someone has said: "Death does not have the last word—life does. Sin does not have the last word—grace does. Darkness does not have the last word—light does. Evil does not have the last word—goodness does."

■ How do you see that playing out in this story? How have you experienced that in your own life?

As you bring your time to a close, take some time to thank God for the many ways God's grace was abundant in your life, despite your failures.

Unit 1

Four World-Changing Days

Session Outcome

To encourage people to decide to follow Jesus and continue in their faith journey with Him.

Customize:

Spirit is the password to access expanded teaching helps on FoundryLeader.com.

Discover:

Illustrated Bible Life digs into the history of Pontius Pilate, Roman prefect of the province of Judea, and provides verse-by-verse commentary on the Scripture passage.

March

26

WHAT WILL YOU DECIDE ABOUT JESUS?

Every person must make a choice to either accept or reject Jesus Christ.

THE WORD

MARK 14:60-64

Then the high priest stood up before them and asked Jesus, "Are you not going to answer? What is this testimony that these men are bringing against you?" ⁶¹But Jesus remained silent and gave no answer.

Again the high priest asked him, "Are you the Messiah, the Son of the Blessed One?"

⁶²"I am," said Jesus. "And you will see the Son of Man sitting at the right hand of the Mighty One and coming on the clouds of heaven."

⁶³The high priest tore his clothes. "Why do we need any more witnesses?" he asked. ⁶⁴"You have heard the blasphemy. What do you think?"

15:2-15

²"Are you the king of the Jews?" asked Pilate.

"You have said so," Jesus replied.

³The chief priests accused him of many things. ⁴So again Pilate asked him, "Aren't you going to answer? See how many things they are accusing you of."

⁵But Jesus still made no reply, and Pilate was amazed.

⁶Now it was the custom at the festival to release a prisoner whom the people requested. ⁷A man called Barabbas was in prison with the insurrectionists who had committed murder in the uprising. ⁸The crowd came up and asked Pilate to do for them what he usually did.

⁹"Do you want me to release to you the king of the Jews?" asked Pilate, ¹⁰knowing it was out of self-interest that the chief priests had

We saw that spiritual failure can and does happen, but it does not need to be final.

This Week:

We will see that every person must make a decision to either receive or refuse Jesus as Lord and Savior.

Notes:

_____

_____

_____

_____

_____

_____

_____

_____

_____

_____

_____

_____

_____

_____

_____

_____

_____

Session 4

handed Jesus over to him. ¹¹But the chief priests stirred up the crowd to have Pilate release Barabbas instead.

KEY VERSE ¹²**"What shall I do, then, with the one you call the king of the Jews?" Pilate asked them.**

¹³"Crucify him!" they shouted.

¹⁴"Why? What crime has he committed?" asked Pilate.

But they shouted all the louder, "Crucify him!"

¹⁵Wanting to satisfy the crowd, Pilate released Barabbas to them. He had Jesus flogged, and handed him over to be crucified.

ENGAGE THE WORD

FALSE ACCUSATION OF BLASPHEMY

Mark 14:60-64

In the previous verses, the leaders brought false witnesses to incriminate Jesus. The use of false witnesses revealed this trial was actually about the claim that Jesus was the Son of God and not about any supposed illegal behavior of Jesus. Even though their false accusations did not agree, the high priest summoned Jesus to defend himself against the charges. Jesus silently refused to respond.

Throughout Mark's gospel, Jesus was hesitant to speak plainly about His identity as the Messiah. He even prevented the evil spirits whom He cast out from proclaiming His identity as the "Holy One of God" (2:24). As the council paraded a lineup of false witnesses against Him, Jesus did not defend himself. Jesus' silence is sometimes difficult to understand. Perhaps He did not want to dignify their false accusations with a reply. Or perhaps He understood any response would be futile because His accusers were already determined to put Him to death (14:55). Mark most likely noted Jesus' silence as a fulfillment of Scripture (see Isaiah 53:7, "As a sheep before its shearers is silent, so he did not open his mouth.").

When the high priest directly asked Jesus if He was the Messiah, the Son of God, Jesus ended His silence with the clear affirmation, "I am." Jesus often spoke of himself with the mysterious title "Son of Man." After affirming His identity, Jesus declared, "And you will see

🔊 **Listen:**

FoundryLeader.com: Who was Pontius Pilate? This week's *Illustrated Bible Life* "Article Out Loud" examines what we know about the Roman leader who turned Jesus over to be crucified.

Notes:

_____

_____

_____

_____

_____

_____

_____

_____

_____

_____

_____

_____

_____

_____

_____

_____

_____

Did You Know?

The phrase "Son of the Blessed One" means "Son of God."
The Jews often avoided the name of God in order to avoid breaking the third commandment (taking God's name in vain).

ACCUSATIONS AND SILENCE

the Son of Man sitting at the right hand of the Mighty One and coming on the clouds of heaven" (v. 62). Jesus' words combined a messianic passage from Psalm 110 with an apocalyptic passage of judgment from Daniel 7. His words prophesied a coming time when the roles would be reversed so that those who were now judging would be judged. For the high priest, this was the last straw. On a trumped up charge of blasphemy, the council and the high priest judged Him worthy of death.

Mark 15:2-5

Roman law forbade local councils from carrying out the death penalty. Therefore, they brought Jesus to Pilate, the Roman military governor over Judea, for trial and questioning. As Jesus appeared before Pilate bound by chains and bloodied by His own Jewish compatriots, Pilate sarcastically asked, "Are you the king of the Jews?" The question itself was serious because the Romans viewed any claim of kingship as a crime against the sovereign authority of Rome. But the circumstances were pathetically ridiculous since the Jews themselves were the ones who had rejected and condemned Jesus.

Much to Pilate's surprise, Jesus responded with a noncommittal answer similar to something like, "Whatever you say." Even when the chief priests piled more unfounded accusations against Him, Jesus remained silent. Pilate called Jesus to defend himself against His accusers, but Jesus refused. Once again, Jesus' silence is difficult to explain except perhaps as a fulfillment of Scripture. In Mark's gospel, Jesus did not speak again until He was on the cross in 15:34.

CHOICE OF JESUS OR BARABBAS

Mark 15:6-15

Mark noted that the crowd asked Pilate to release a prisoner, as was the custom at such a festival like Passover. Pilate knew it was out of envy and self-interest that the chief priests had arrested and charged

Discover:

At the end of Mark's gospel, we discover a powerful character named Pontius Pilate. This Roman leader is so intertwined with Jesus' trial and ultimate sentencing to death that his name appears in some of the most famous and widely-quoted creeds of the Christian church. How did Pontius Pilate end up in this story? Let's find out in this week's *Illustrated Bible Life* article, "Pontius Pilate."

Think About It

By exchanging Barabbas for Jesus, the Jewish religious leaders rejected Jesus, the true Son of the Father, and replaced Him with Barabbas, whose name means literally "a son of a father."

Jesus (v. 10). He undoubtedly viewed the prisoner release as the perfect opportunity to defuse the situation, gain the favor of the crowd, and release Jesus, who was obviously innocent of any wrongdoing.

This was where the infamous criminal Barabbas entered the picture. One needs to recognize the significant irony present in this tragic account. Whereas Jesus was falsely accused as a rebel who was vying for Jewish kingship, Barabbas was a renowned political revolutionary who was guilty of murder in his attempts to challenge and overthrow the Roman authority. Likewise, the chief priests accused and condemned Jesus for claiming He was the Son of God the Father while they sought the release of Barabbas, whose name literally means "a son of a father." Being quick to condemn the innocent Jesus for crimes He never committed, they were equally as quick to exonerate the guilty Barabbas for crimes he had assuredly committed. Anticipating Pilate's offer to release a prisoner during the festival, the chief priests stirred up the crowd to demand Barabbas' release while also demanding Jesus' death.

Pilate tried to reason with the crowd by challenging them to identify any crime Jesus committed, but they only shouted all the louder for Jesus to be crucified. The verdict of the crowd, at the instigation of the Jewish religious leaders, was a travesty of justice, baseless, and without merit. Based on peer pressure alone, they rejected and condemned Jesus without even knowing or considering Him. Similarly, Pilate condemned Jesus merely out of the selfish desire to satisfy the crowd and gain their favor. Therefore, he released Barabbas, had Jesus beaten, and handed Jesus over to be crucified.

REFLECT Who is Jesus and what have you decided about Him?

DANIEL G. POWERS

Notes:

_____

_____

_____

_____

_____

_____

_____

_____

_____

_____

_____

_____

_____

_____

_____

_____

_____

_____

Discussion Guide

Connect to My Experience

Pretend for a moment that an alien has just landed on earth and you have been tasked with helping the alien understand earth's culture. This would mean trying to describe things that you may have never had to describe before. How would you describe: ice cream, democracy, television, cell phones, and music?

In society today, there are many who do not know much, if anything, about Jesus.

- ◼ How would you describe Jesus to someone who didn't know Jesus?

- ◼ What would you tell this person about your decision to follow Jesus? What was happening in your life at that time?

- ◼ What do you think keeps people from believing/accepting Jesus today?

Transition:

In today's text, we encounter several people deciding what they will do with Jesus. Yet the question remains for us, what will we do with Jesus?

Connect to the Word

Invite someone to read Mark 14:60-64, then discuss the following,

The Sanhedrin was the highest tribunal of the Jews. Mark 14:55 tells us that "the chief priests and the whole Sanhedrin were looking for evidence against Jesus so that they could put him to death." The religious leaders brought in false witnesses to testify against Jesus. The high priest demanded that Jesus respond to their accusations against Him.

- ◼ If you were being falsely accused, would you be able to remain silent? Why or why not? How would you react if your life was on the line?

- ◼ Why do you think Jesus remained silent in response to the high priest's questions?

The high priest gets to the heart of the matter and the heart of Jesus' identity, asking again, "Are you the Messiah, the Son of the Blessed One?"

- ◼ How does Jesus respond to this specific question? Why do you think He gives an answer here and not to the prior question? (The time had arrived for Him to reveal that He was the Messiah.)

- ◼ Why does Jesus' expounded answer cause such anger in the high priest? (Jesus says that they, the religious leaders, will see His elevated status. He will be vindicated by the Mighty One, thus proving their actions worthless. Jesus will return as Judge over those who are now judging Him.)

- ◼ What had the high priest decided about Jesus? (He rejected Jesus as the Messiah, the Son of God.)

- ◼ What stands out to you most from this verbal exchange between the high priest and Jesus? Why?

Invite someone to read Mark 15:2-5, then discuss the following,

The Jewish authorities had reached a decision: Jesus was worthy of death for blasphemy, but they could not act upon their decision because they could not impose the death penalty. Roman authority would not convict Jesus of blasphemy, so the religious leaders' charges were translated into political ones.

- ◼ Why do you think Jesus answers Pilate's question in the way He does, saying, "You have said so"? What does Jesus' answer convey?

- ◼ What do you think Pilate understood by the title "king" and how does that

Insight

The Sanhedrin was the highest tribunal of the Jews. It consisted of the high priest, any former high priests, members of the high priestly family, and elders and scribes. It had definite meeting times and was presided over by the high priest. It was their custom to sit in a semicircle. The total membership numbered 71, including the high priest. It had authority to make arrests, and it could judge cases that did not involve capital punishment.

Invite someone to read Mark 15:6-15, then discuss the following,

compare to Jesus' understanding of kingship? How does Jesus' current behavior reveal what kind of king He is?

■ In what ways is Jesus' kingdom different from the Roman concept of kingdom?

Our third accusatory party, the crowd, enters the scene. Pilate offers the crowd a choice.

■ What kind of person was Barabbas (v. 7)? In Pilate's mind, do you think he thought of Jesus and Barabbas in the same way—being insurrectionists? (He knew Jesus was there because of the envy of the chief priests.)

■ What informed the crowd's behavior? (see v.11) Are crowds generally prone to reason? Why did Barabbas' release win out?

■ How does the crowd respond when Pilate asks, "What crime has [Jesus] committed?" What does this tell us about the crowd?

■ Is there ever a danger for us as believers to get caught up in a "crowd" mentality? If so, in what way?

■ We are told that Pilate "wanted to satisfy the crowd." What does this tell us about Pilate? Are we ever tempted in wanting to satisfy the crowd? If so, how? How can we resist that kind of temptation?

■ All three accusatory parties decided against Jesus. How could things have gone differently for the high priest, for Pilate, and for the crowd? (They could have accepted Jesus as the Messiah.)

Connect to My Life and the World

Bring your session to a close with the following discussion:

■ If you could summarize the motive for each party who decided against Jesus in this passage, what would you say led each to their decision: high priest, Pilate, crowd.

Each day we encounter people or messages that are contrary to the message of the gospel. They deny Jesus by the things they say and/or do.

■ How can we resist the cultural "crowds" that attempt to lead us to deny Jesus?

■ How are people forming their decisions today about Jesus? Do you think Jesus can get a fair hearing? Why, or why not?

Think about your life.

■ How would you finish this sentence: I follow Jesus today because _____?

Think about the church.

■ In what ways can the church go against the cultural crowds and proclaim the truth of Jesus to their community?

Think about others.

■ How can you encourage others to follow Jesus?

Close in prayer.

Unit 1

Four World-Changing Days

Session Outcome

To help the people understand afresh the meaning of Jesus' suffering and death.

Customize:

Spirit is the password to access expanded teaching helps on FoundryLeader.com.

Discover:

Illustrated Bible Life examines the meaning behind the tearing of the temple curtain at Jesus' death on the cross, and gives verse-by-verse commentary on the Scripture passage.

April

2

CHRIST CRUCIFIED

Every element associated with the death of Jesus provides insight into our Lord's identity, mission, and significance.

THE WORD

MARK 15:21-39

A certain man from Cyrene, Simon, the father of Alexander and Rufus, was passing by on his way in from the country, and they forced him to carry the cross. ²²They brought Jesus to the place called Golgotha (which means "the place of the skull"). ²³Then they offered him wine mixed with myrrh, but he did not take it. ²⁴And they crucified him. Dividing up his clothes, they cast lots to see what each would get.

²⁵It was nine in the morning when they crucified him. ²⁶The written notice of the charge against him read: the king of the jews.

²⁷They crucified two rebels with him, one on his right and one on his left. [28] ²⁹Those who passed by hurled insults at him, shaking their heads and saying, "So! You who are going to destroy the temple and build it in three days, ³⁰come down from the cross and save yourself!" ³¹In the same way the chief priests and the teachers of the law mocked him among themselves. "He saved others," they said, "but he can't save himself! ³²Let this Messiah, this king of Israel, come down now from the cross, that we may see and believe." Those crucified with him also heaped insults on him.

³³At noon, darkness came over the whole land until three in the afternoon. ³⁴And at three in the afternoon Jesus cried out in a loud voice, "Eloi, Eloi, lema sabachthani?" (which means "My God, my God, why have you forsaken me?").

³⁵When some of those standing near heard this, they said, "Listen, he's calling Elijah."

³⁶Someone ran, filled a sponge with wine vinegar, put it on a

Last Week:

We recognized the need to make a decision about what we believe about Jesus.

This Week:

We will recognize the mighty power of God in the cross.

staff, and offered it to Jesus to drink. "Now leave him alone. Let's see if Elijah comes to take him down," he said.

³⁷With a loud cry, Jesus breathed his last.

³⁸The curtain of the temple was torn in two from top to bottom.

KEY VERSE **³⁹And when the centurion, who stood there in front of Jesus, saw how he died, he said, "Surely this man was the Son of God!"**

ENGAGE THE WORD

CRUCIFIED AS KING OF THE JEWS

Mark 15:21-27

Normally, those condemned to death by crucifixion would carry their own cross (or the crossbeam) to the site of their death. Mark did not explain why Jesus could not carry His cross, but the reason was undoubtedly connected to the brutal beating inflicted on Him by the soldiers (15:19). Little is known about Simon of Cyrene, who was forced to carry Jesus' cross. Nonetheless, his role is a powerful example of the moment in every believer's life when the cross of Jesus becomes our cross, which we must take up to follow Him (Mark 8:34-38).

Myrrh mixed with wine was sometimes used to dull pain, but the addition of myrrh would make the wine virtually undrinkable. The offer of undrinkable mixture to still Jesus' great thirst was probably another form of sadistic mockery aimed at Jesus. But Jesus refused to drink. At the Last Supper, Jesus declared He would not drink from the fruit of the vine until He would drink it again in the kingdom of God (14:25). Here in His own valley of the shadow of death, Jesus was determined to remain fully conscious as He accepted His suffering for the sake of all humanity.

Executioners often took the clothes and other sparse belongings of their victims, sometimes casting lots to determine who would receive them. Mark undoubtedly recognized this detail as a fulfillment of Psalm 22:18. Psalm 22 has been recognized as portraying a vivid picture of suffering that is remarkably similar to Jesus' own suffering. Mark alluded to this psalm again in verse 20 (Psalm 22:7) and in verse 34 (Psalm 22:1).

Notes:

_____

_____

_____

_____

_____

_____

_____

_____

_____

_____

_____

_____

_____

_____

_____

_____

_____

🔊 **Listen:**

FoundryLeader.com: Why did the temple curtain tear when Jesus took His last breath on the cross? That's the question in this week's *Illustrated Bible Life* "Article Out Loud."

Notes:

_____

_____

_____

_____

_____

_____

_____

_____

_____

_____

_____

_____

_____

_____

_____

_____

_____

_____

Did You Know?

It was 9 AM, the third hour, when Jesus was crucified (v. 25). At high noon, the sixth hour (v. 33) an unusual darkness covered the land, as prophesied (Amos 8:9). It was 3 PM, the ninth hour (v. 34), which was the Jewish hour of prayer, when Jesus expressed His agony and quoted from Psalm 22 in prayer.

MOCKING INSULTS

THIS MAN WAS THE SON OF GOD!

As was customary, Jesus' supposed crime was written on a placard and attached to the cross: "The king of the Jews." Pilate undoubtedly created this message as an ironic insult to the Jewish leaders who had coerced him into executing Jesus. For the Christian, however, no truer words have ever been written. Crucified between two criminals, Jesus was "numbered with the transgressors" (Isaiah 53:12).

Mark 15:29-32

The bystanders hurled insults at Jesus, shaking their heads in contempt. The taunts and mocking echoed the words of Psalm 22:7. Scornfully, the crowd challenged Jesus to come down from the cross and save himself. Similarly, the Jewish religious leaders mocked Jesus, saying, "He saved others but He can't save himself." With contempt they called Him "Messiah" and "king of Israel," and they, too, challenged Him to come down from the cross that they might see and believe.

The derision of the bystanders was deeply ironic for Mark. Their mocking words testified to an incredible truth far beyond their comprehension. Jesus' death was a "ransom" for others (10:45), and in order to save others He must not and could not save himself. As humiliation, indignity, and insult were piled upon Jesus, the true Messiah and King of Israel endured the derision with resolution, endurance, and determination. After all, Jesus had taught His followers to "take up" the cross, not to "come down" from one. In obedience and submission to God's plan for the salvation of others, Jesus did not turn away from the cross.

Mark 15:33-39

At noon, darkness covered the land, coinciding with the last three hours of Jesus' suffering. The prophet Amos had written, "'In that day,' declares the Sovereign Lord, 'I will make the sun go down at noon and darken the earth in broad daylight'" (8:9). Amos' "day of the Lord" was a day of judgment against those who per-

Discover:

When Jesus died, the curtain of the temple was torn from top to bottom (Mark 15:38). This curious event is not only associated directly with Jesus' death, but carries tremendous historical and theological symbolism that heightens the significance of Jesus' suffering and death for the forgiveness of sin. Learn more in this week's *Illustrated Bible Life* article, "The Tearing of the Temple Curtain."

Notes:

Session 5

Think About It

While it would appear that God's power and purposes were frustrated by the death of His Son Jesus, the ironic reality is that God's power and purposes were indelibly displayed and eternally established through the obedience of the Son to the Father. On that fateful day, Jesus became the Mediator of salvation to all who would believe in Him.

verted justice (Amos 5:18-24), an idea that Mark could easily apply to the circumstances of Jesus' death.

At the height of His pain, Jesus exclaimed, "My God, my God, why have you forsaken me?" Some interpret this as a reflection of Jesus' intense suffering, while others view it as an expression of His full identification with sinful humanity and the Father's abandonment of Him. Others point to Jesus' exclamation as a quotation from Psalm 22:1, which begins with forsaken anguish, but ends in vindication (vv. 22-31). Thus, Jesus' agonized cry in the midst of His suffering might reflect a confident trust that His suffering and death would be ultimately vindicated by God the Father. There is undoubtedly an element of truth reflected in each of these suggestions. Jesus' agonized cry reflected the intense suffering and dreadfulness caused by His full identification with sinful humanity, but it also reflected His confident hope of His Father's vindication. With a final loud cry, Jesus took His last breath and He died.

With two short emphatic sentences, Mark summed up the incredible result of Jesus' death. First, the temple curtain that separated the holy place from the holy of holies was torn from top to bottom. This was undeniably an act of God, whose presence was now relocated in the crucified and soon-to-be risen Christ. The presence of God would no longer be contained and hidden in the temple.

Second, the centurion declared that Jesus was indeed the Son of God. This declaration is the ultimate climax of Mark's entire gospel. Salvation would no longer be determined by membership in the bloodline of the Jews through Abraham. Instead, salvation would be offered to anyone—even a Roman centurion!—who believed in Jesus as the Son of God. Jesus' work was finished.

REFLECT Take time to think about the message of the cross.

DANIEL G. POWERS

Discussion Guide

Connect to My Experience	Everywhere you look there are symbols. A symbol is an image that stands for or represents something else.

- What are some famous symbols? (smiley face, flags, peace sign)
- What are familiar symbols we see each day? (traffic signs, parking signs, consumer product logos, and so on)
- What are symbols we use in the church?
- At the center of Christian worship is a Savior who died on a cross. Why do you think the symbol of the cross is so significant?

Transition:

The cross is a powerful symbol. Today's session reminds us that Jesus' death on the cross reveals God's identity and mission, and calls us to consider anew our identity and mission as God's people.

Connect to the Word

Invite someone to read Mark 15:21-27, then discuss the following,

Pilate handed Jesus over to be crucified (15:15).

- We are told a man named Simon was forced to carry Jesus' cross. Why was Jesus so weak that He could not carry the weight of the cross? (Jesus was beaten and physically abused.)
- Scholars tell us that the inclusion of a person's name in a biblical account is significant. Why do you think Mark goes through the effort to include the names of Simon, Alexander, and Rufus? What is their role in this story?

Myrrh mixed with wine was a sedative. Jesus refused to drink it.

- What does this tell us about Jesus? (He chose to feel the full weight of suffering.)

Have someone read Psalm 22.

- How would you describe the mood of Psalm 22? How does the psalm conclude?
- After reading that, would you still say that the soldiers are in charge of the action?
- How does this psalm help you understand the events of Jesus' crucifixion?
- What is the point of the written charge against Jesus in Mark 15:26? Is there irony in this charge against Jesus?

Invite someone to read Mark 15:29-32, then discuss the following,

Mark's gospel tells of three groups who mocked Jesus as He hung on the cross: "those who passed by" (v. 29), "the chief priests and teachers of the law" (v. 31), and "those crucified with him" (v. 32b).

- Based on the insults being hurled at Jesus, how did the passersby and religious leaders understand power? According to them, if Jesus really was the Messiah, what should He have been able to do?

Some who passed by and some religious leaders suggest that Jesus should come down from the cross and save himself.

- How does this suggestion and attempted mockery fail to see who Jesus was

Insight

At the time, the cross seemed to be a symbol of weakness. It seemed to say the enemies of Jesus had won. But now it is the center piece of Christianity and a symbol of God's power for victory over temptation, sin, and eternal death. It brings a response of praise and celebration.

and the nature of His kingdom? ("Jesus taught His followers to 'take up' the cross, not to 'come down' from one.")

Jesus is first insulted by the crowd and then the religious leaders. This section concludes with those crucified with Jesus heaping insults upon Him (v.32).

- ▢ Why does Mark include this detail? (Everyone has taken to insulting Him; Jesus can't even find consolation among those being killed next to Him.)

- ▢ In what ways do people today insult Jesus anew? In what ways do cultural voices mock the gospel message?

Invite someone to read Mark 15:33-39, then discuss the following,

Perhaps the most painful part of this section is Jesus' cry of "My God, my God, why have you forsaken me?"

- ▢ Why do you think Jesus uttered those words? Why doesn't Mark provide any explanation as to the meaning?

- ▢ Did God actually abandon Jesus at the cross? Why or why not? (Share: Jesus was quoting Psalm 22:1. The words seem to indicate that God had left Jesus, due to God's holy nature and Jesus' weight of sin He carried on the cross. However, the New Testament says clearly that God in Christ was reconciling the world to himself—they were in this together. But Jesus did experience the feelings of loneliness and isolation. The inner agony Jesus suffered on our behalf far outweighed the intense outer agony He endured.)

- ▢ Why is it significant that the curtain of the temple was torn in two, from top to bottom? (The separation between God and humanity was bridged by Jesus' death. See Hebrews 10:19-20, 22a.)

The verb Mark uses here to describe the tearing of the curtain is the same verb he used to describe the heavens being torn open and the Spirit landing on Jesus in 1:10.

- ▢ How might that shape our understanding of what is happening here?

- ▢ In the final verse (v. 39), who is it that correctly grasps Jesus' identity?

Connect to My Life and the World

Bring your session to a close by discussing the following:

- ▢ Is Jesus' death consistent with the way He lived His life? If so, how?

- ▢ How did Jesus respond to those who mocked, ridiculed, and ultimately put Him to death? Was Jesus unique in His ability to withstand such contempt, or are believers today called to respond in a similar way?

- ▢ Like Jesus on the cross, have you ever felt abandoned by God? What was going on in your life at that time? How did you recover a sense of God's presence in your life? What would you say to someone who was feeling that way today?

- ▢ If you had to describe what the kingdom of God is like only through the lens of this crucifixion story, what would you say?

Close in prayer.

Unit 1

Four World-Changing Days

Session Outcome

To affirm that the resurrection of Jesus means victory over death and life everlasting.

Customize:

Spirit is the password to access expanded teaching helps on FoundryLeader.com.

Discover:

Illustrated Bible Life looks at the final chapter of Mark, and gives verse-by-verse commentary on the Scripture passage.

April

9

CHRIST ALIVE

In the resurrection, Jesus Christ achieved victory over sin and death.

THE WORD

MARK 15:42-47

It was Preparation Day (that is, the day before the Sabbath). So as evening approached, ⁴³Joseph of Arimathea, a prominent member of the Council, who was himself waiting for the kingdom of God, went boldly to Pilate and asked for Jesus' body. ⁴⁴Pilate was surprised to hear that he was already dead. Summoning the centurion, he asked him if Jesus had already died. ⁴⁵When he learned from the centurion that it was so, he gave the body to Joseph. ⁴⁶So Joseph bought some linen cloth, took down the body, wrapped it in the linen, and placed it in a tomb cut out of rock. Then he rolled a stone against the entrance of the tomb. ⁴⁷Mary Magdalene and Mary the mother of Joseph saw where he was laid.

16:1-8

¹When the Sabbath was over, Mary Magdalene, Mary the mother of James, and Salome bought spices so that they might go to anoint Jesus' body. ²Very early on the first day of the week, just after sunrise, they were on their way to the tomb ³and they asked each other, "Who will roll the stone away from the entrance of the tomb?"

⁴But when they looked up, they saw that the stone, which was very large, had been rolled away. ⁵As they entered the tomb, they saw a young man dressed in a white robe sitting on the right side, and they were alarmed.

KEY VERSE ⁶**"Don't be alarmed," he said. "You are looking for Jesus the Nazarene, who was crucified. He has risen! He is not here. See the place where they laid him.** ⁷But go, tell his disciples and Peter, 'He is going ahead of you into Galilee. There you will see him, just as he told you.'"

We learned of the power of the cross.

We will learn of the power of the resurrection of Jesus.

Notes:

_____

_____

_____

Session 6

⁸Trembling and bewildered, the women went out and fled from the tomb. They said nothing to anyone, because they were afraid.

_____

ENGAGE THE WORD

THE BURIAL OF JESUS

Mark 15:42-47

_____

Mark narrated the burial of Jesus with simple and unembellished details that underscore the certainty of His death. Death by crucifixion often stretched out over several days as the victim would slowly deteriorate, dehydrate, and bleed out on the cross. The Romans often left a decaying body on a cross as a warning and deterrent against other potential rebels against the state. But Jewish custom required burial before sunset to prevent pollution of the land (Deuteronomy 21:23).

_____

_____

Jesus' death occurred in the afternoon, only hours before sunset and the beginning of the Sabbath. Typically, family or friends requested the body for burial, but Jesus' family and friends had abandoned Him.

_____

Mark observed that it was Preparation Day, the day before the Sabbath, to emphasize the hasty preparations that surrounded the burial of Jesus. This reference could also be a subtle foreshadowing that God was preparing a resurrection that would radically transform the significance of Jesus' death.

_____

_____

A pious Jew named Joseph asked Pilate for Jesus' body for burial. Little is known about Joseph's background or motivation, but he was possibly a secret follower of Jesus since Mark noted he was "waiting for the kingdom of God." Since death by crucifixion was usually a lengthy affair, Pilate expressed surprise to hear that Jesus had already died. When the Roman centurion confirmed the death of Jesus, Pilate released the body to Joseph, who quickly took down the body, wrapped it in linen cloth, and placed it in a stone crypt that had been cut into the rock. He rolled a large stone in front of the opening of the tomb to protect the body from wild animals or intruders. Mark recorded that two women watched (literally, "were

_____

_____

_____

_____

Listen:

FoundryLeader.com: How did Mark intend for his gospel to end? That's the focus of this week's *Illustrated Bible Life* "Article Out Loud."

Notes:

_____

_____

_____

_____

_____

_____

_____

_____

_____

_____

_____

_____

_____

_____

_____

_____

_____

Did You Know?

To seal a tomb, a flat, rounded stone was placed in a sloping channel dug at the base of the entrance. The stone could be rolled easily down the slope across the entrance, but would require several people to remove.

WHO WILL ROLL THE STONE AWAY?

watching") these events take place, and they saw where Jesus was buried.

Mark was very careful to note that Jesus was really dead: Joseph announced it, Pilate researched it, the centurion verified it, and the women watched it happen.

Mark 16:1-4

The women followers of Jesus played a surprisingly prominent role at the end of Mark's gospel. Their significance is all the more unexpected because Mark never mentioned anything about women followers of Jesus earlier in his gospel. Nonetheless, when Jesus' family and all His disciples had abandoned Him, these female followers became the first eyewitnesses of the foundational Christian belief that "Jesus died ... was buried . . . and was raised" (1 Corinthians 15:3).

After the Sabbath, a group of three women—Mary Magdalene, Mary the mother of James, and Salome—bought spices to anoint Jesus' body. The hasty timing of Jesus' death and burial before the beginning of the Sabbath at sunset had prevented them from making the arrangements earlier. As they made their way to the tomb after sunrise on that first Easter Sunday morning, their thoughts were occupied with the dilemma of removing the stone that blocked the entrance to the tomb. Despite Jesus' repeated prophecies that He would die and be raised again on the third day (Mark 8:31; 9:31; 10:34), this expectation was nowhere in their thoughts. Instead, they worried about the stone that sealed the grave.

As often happens, the things people worry about the most never actually materialize. When the women approached the tomb and looked up at the entrance, they saw that the large stone had already been rolled away. Mark did not identify specifically who or how the stone had been moved, but the passive voice ("had been moved") in Scripture is often used as a "divine passive" to describe an act of God. Indeed, what

Discover:

Anyone who has read an English translation of Mark's gospel published in the past 50 years has encountered the problem with the ending. Every modern translation states that some ancient manuscripts end with 16:8, while other ancient manuscripts contain verses 9-20. Just how did Mark end his gospel? Let's take a closer look in this week's *Illustrated Bible Life* article, "How Did Mark End His Gospel?"

Notes:

Think About It

Mark's report of women as prime witnesses of Jesus' resurrection oddly attests to the reliability of his account. Since women were considered unreliable witnesses, Mark would hardly have invented them as his primary source.

JESUS HAS RISEN!

man (or in this case, "women") could not do, God did: He rolled the stone away!

Mark 16:5-8

Since the entrance to the tomb was open, the women went inside to anoint Jesus' body. But the body was not there. Instead, they saw a "young man dressed in a white robe" sitting just to the right of where the body had lain. The reference to the white robe agrees with Matthew's account that this was an angel with clothes that were "white as snow" (Matthew 28:3). As one might expect, the women were greatly alarmed, probably as much from the absence of the body as from the presence of the angelic young man.

After calming their fears, the white-clad messenger delivered three important truths that continue to encourage and inspire followers of Jesus even today. First, Jesus is risen! He is not in the grave. The tomb is empty, and Jesus is alive! Second, Jesus has gone ahead of you. Not only did He go ahead of them into Galilee (14:28), where He would meet His disciples, but He goes ahead of every believer as a divine "Way maker" through life towards heaven. Third, you will see Him again. This promise must have ignited the fires of hope in the hearts of the disciples. Specifically, the disciples saw the resurrected Jesus in Galilee, just as the angel said. But the day is also coming when all creation will see the resurrected Jesus when He returns in glory and honor. This promise of seeing Jesus again continues to prompt hope and faith that we too will meet our Lord in the future. This is because Jesus is risen; He is risen indeed!

REFLECT Think about what "He is risen; He is risen indeed!" means to you.

DANIEL G. POWERS

Discussion Guide

Connect to My Experience

We have all experienced something that we would consider "life-changing."

- ◼ What does it mean for something to be life-changing?

- ◼ What events in your life's journey have been life-changing for you? Was it a positive or negative experience?

- ◼ How did your life change as a result of this particular event? How did it impact your day-to-day living?

Transition:

In today's session, we recall the most life-changing event—the resurrection of Jesus—and celebrate God's victory over sin and death.

Connect to the Word

Invite someone to read Mark 15:42-47, then discuss the following,

Jesus has died and Joseph of Arimathea asks Pilate for Jesus' body. Joseph was a rich man and a secret (John 19:38) follower of Jesus (Matthew 27:57). He was a member of the Council, a good and upright man (Luke 23:50-53).

- ◼ Why do you think boldness was required for Joseph to approach Pilate to ask for Jesus' body?

- ◼ Is there a lesson we can learn from Joseph of Arimathea? If so, what? (He was good and upright, but a secret follower before Jesus' death. Now, after Jesus' death, he becomes bold.)

Verse 44 says that Pilate was surprised to learn that Jesus was already dead. They most likely anticipated a slow death so it could serve as a warning to others to not challenge their authority.

- ◼ What clues are we given that tell us Jesus really was dead? (Pilate hears of it; Centurion confirms it; Joseph takes possession of Jesus' body; Joseph transports Jesus' body to a tomb; the tomb is enclosed by a large stone; Mary Magdalene and another Mary witness see where Jesus was laid)

- ◼ Why is it necessary for Mark to put so much emphasis on the reality of Jesus being dead? (Jesus in fact did die.)

- ◼ Why does verse 47 reveal that the two Marys saw where Jesus was laid? (they are being established as witnesses; they did not flee like everyone else)

Invite someone to read Mark 16:1-4, then discuss the following,

Salome has now joined Mary and Mary and the three of them have assembled to anoint Jesus' body.

- ◼ What do we know about them and what do their actions reveal about them? (Mary Magdalene: Jesus had driven out demons from her [Luke 8:2]; Mary mother of James: James was one of the disciples; Salome: mother of James and John. Their actions show love and concern for Jesus.)

- ◼ What clues do we have that the women experienced something extraordinary as they approached the tomb?

- ◼ How does Mark reinforce in these verses that Jesus really was dead?

Invite someone to read Mark 16:5-8, then discuss the following,

Verse 5 says that upon entering the tomb and seeing a young man dressed in a white robe, the women were alarmed.

Insight

The resurrection is not a legendary story; it is not a fairy tale; it is not simply a product of the gospel writer's attempt to put a happy ending on a tragic story. The resurrection happened and because God raised His Son to life again, everything has changed. We need not fear that anger, hate, and sin are more powerful than love, mercy, and grace. We need not wonder if Jesus is who He claimed to be. The resurrection defines our faith.

- What was the cause of their alarm?

- What are the three important announcements the young man makes to the women? (Jesus is risen; Jesus will go ahead of them; you will see Him again)

- How does Mark say the women responded to this news? How would you have responded?

Scholars note that the testimony of women was not highly valued in that culture, thus the inclusion of the women as witnesses of the resurrection gives further weight to the reliability of their testimony.

- What does that tell us about the nature of God's kingdom and mission?

Finally, we have to note that the angel makes a point of telling the women that they are to go to Jesus' disciples "and Peter" (v.7).

- What is the purpose of singling Peter out? Why is this important in this resurrection story? (See 14:66-72.)

- What key words do we find in verses 6-7? (see, go, tell) How are these three words applied to our spiritual lives today? (We are called to experience (see) the transformational power of Jesus and, in turn, enter (go) our world and share (tell) the good news of the gospel.)

Connect to My Life and the World

Today's story involved different types of people, but each one had an encounter with Christ.

- As you think about the people in today's story, how does their story resonate with yours? In what ways are you encountering the risen Christ?

One thing we encounter in this text is the women worrying about how they'll move the stone in front of the tomb; yet at the same time God was doing something they never could have imagined.

- What is it that causes you concern today?

- How does this story speak to you in the midst of your concern and anxiety?

Sometimes in our lives we don't find God in the places where we thought God would be, but God has gone ahead of us and is doing a new thing.

- Have you ever experienced this in your life? If so, how?

The young man dressed in white in the tomb announces three important truths: Jesus has risen, Jesus has gone ahead, and we will see Jesus again.

- What comfort do you find in these life-changing, world altering truths?

Jesus' resurrection has cosmic implications, yet the young man dressed in white had a very personal message for Peter.

- What does this mean to you? In the midst of all that is going on in the world today, what do you think Jesus wants you to know about your life with Him?

Were it not for the resurrection of Jesus, you would not be gathered today in this group. But Jesus is risen!

- How has the resurrection of Jesus been life-changing for you?

As you close, give God thanks for the new life God has given to you.

Unit 2 Introduction

Introduction to the Book of James

*B*e you doers and not just hearers of the word (1:22).

Faith without works is dead (1:26).

Draw near to God and He will draw near to you (4:8).

Resist the devil and he will flee from you (4:7).

Consider it pure joy, my brothers and sisters, whenever you face trials of many kinds (1:2).

Confess your sins to each other and pray for each other so that you may be healed. The prayer of a righteous person is powerful and effective (5:16).

Is anyone among you in trouble? Let them pray. Is anyone happy? Let them sing songs of praise (5:13).

If any of you lacks wisdom, you should ask God, who gives generously to all without finding fault, and it will be given to you (1:5).

Blessed is the one who perseveres under trial because, having stood the test, that person will receive the crown of life that the Lord has promised to those who love him (1:12).

These verses from the book of James highlight the strong and powerful writing of the book, perhaps the New Testament's greatest challenge to authentic Christian living. Most who read them will acknowledge that they have often failed the test. The book of James is written to inspire believers to live lives of holiness, a witness to the grace of God that saves them.

The book of James is possibly the earliest writing in all the New Testament. Scholars believe James was written by the half-brother of Jesus. He was the one who gave the deciding speech at the Council of Jerusalem in AD 45 (Acts 15) and was regarded as one of the pillars of the early church (Galatians 2:9). The book of James is often referred to as the "Proverbs of the New Testament." Reflecting its likeness to the Wisdom Literature of the Old Testaments, it is regarded throughout Christian history as a "manual" of faithful living that has been used in catechisms and monastic treatises. James borrows liberally from the Old Testament throughout his writing quoting the "Law" from Leviticus 19, and alluding to the Prophets, especially Amos, and the Wisdom Literature of Proverbs 27:1, Ecclesiastes 12:6, and the suffering of Job. Grouped by scholars as one of the "General Epistles" with those written by Peter, John, and Jude, the book of James is written to a general audience of believers wherever they may be and not to one specific church or Christians in one particular city. It contains timeless truths and some of the most powerful advice in all of Scripture concerning the life of faith written to press the faithful into genuine Christian living. James 1:22, "Be you doers and not just hearers of the Word," sets the tone for the entirety of the book.

Divided into five chapters consisting of 108 verses and written in 1742 words, James delivers practical exhortations or strongly-worded encouragement to connect right belief in Christ with right living, orthodoxy to Christian holiness. The five chapters cover a number of Christian discipleship issues and offer practical, straight-forward guidance for those who follow Christ as their Lord. A quick overview of the chapters allows to see them together and consider how best to approach them as we teach.

Chapter 1 follows the theme of living stable Christian lives as we face trials and temptations of many kinds. James calls for authentic living following the example of Christ. Rejoice when you face trials. Let them lead you into a mature, perfected faith. Don't get angry. Reign in your tongue and your speech. Learn to listen and not respond quickly or in haste. Don't give in to doubt or evil desires of your own when temptations come as such things lead to sin. Don't be polluted by the world; instead, practice humility. Do not depend on riches or station in life, but trust in God. Do what He commands and be doers of the Word as this will show faith in God and lead to the good works He gives grace to do. Care for the poor and the widow and receive the blessings of God. Persevere by God's working in you in every circumstance, trial, and temptation and you will receive the crown of life from God.

Chapter 2 captures two themes necessary for holy living. First, do good to everyone regardless of their station in life and how they look. Never show favoritism to anyone. Love everyone because everyone is loved by God. Avoid the temptation to love only those who are easy to love and so fulfill the entirety of the law. Love everyone: young and old, wealthy and poor, easy and difficult. Second, remember that love and good deeds always work together. Avoid the easy distinctions of believing that if you mean well it is okay or if you do something that counts as faith in God. Faith and works are more than intimately connected; they are two sides of the same coin called holiness that always work together. True faith always leads to good works. Good works are always an expression of true faith. Obedience and action are the necessary parts of faith in God. Consider this as you live for God: Faith without works is like a body without a spirit. Faith without works is dead.

Chapter 3 combines proper speech with sincere wisdom. Use your speech to praise God and refrain from cursing others. Consider thoughtfully what you say before you speak. So wisdom in the Christian life is a careful consideration. Just as there are two kinds of speech, blessings and curses, there are two kinds of wisdom, earthly and heavenly. Earthly "wisdom" is based on the senses and can lead to harboring bitterness and anger because we don't see life as fair or someone as worth loving. Heavenly wisdom, on the other hand, is pure and loves peace. Practice peace as it comes from God and your reward is righteousness.

Chapter 4 presents an argument for being obedient to God and living for Him, by His grace, in the present. Be obedient. Follow the commandments and avoid the temptation from within to live for yourself. Do not covet, do not kill, do not slander. Never use what God gives you for evil and worldly pleasure. Further, do not even plan or think about doing such things in the future. Resist the Devil and he will flee from you. Instead, do what God wills and do the good in front of you. If you do not do good, the good that is a gift from God for you to do as you live in the present, it is sin.

Chapter 5 caps the book and brings the whole of it together with the holy advice to never panic, especially when distress or trial comes to you. Practice patience. Think before you act, listen before you speak, consider what God is doing in all things. Use your wealth and whatever you have to help others because it is from God. Pray for the sick and believe as you pray as action that shows your faith in God and it will do much good. Do all the good you can for anyone who wanders away from the faith and love them, show them by your actions that God is love. It will save their life and cover a multitude of sins.

So how should we teach this book full of wisdom and advice on holy living? As you teach, focus on these four touchstones:

1. Exhortation and inspiration: The book of James has been used by preachers and teachers throughout Christian history to inspire complacent believers and congregations and to prod them to good works. Let the Word be your guide. Repeat the verses as you go and get your students to do it with you. Faith without works is dead. Resist the Devil and he will flee from you. Consider it a good thing when you are tempted. We need to hear these words so we will do the good works that God is leading us to. Learn wisdom from such words and let the Word of God inspire believers to holiness, perfection, and loving God and loving others.

2. Connect faith and works: Remember to do the necessary work of connecting the doing of good deeds as a Christian to following the commandments that are the grace of God working in us. Forgetting to do this is the greatest "temptation" in teaching James. James is a full of good theology and we always need to remember that as we teach. Practicing what you preach is a learned skill for Christians called discipleship. Focus on reminding your group members that knowing and doing, believing and practicing are two sides of the same coin called Christian holiness.

3. Connect the dots: James, though a short book and filled with "sound bite" theology, should always be taught remembering all of it as you explore the individual parts. Do the theological work of connecting the verses that stick out like "Faith without works is dead" or "Do not slander others" with the Sermon on the Mount from Jesus, the Ten Commandments, and the Wisdom Literature of the Old Testament. The verses are timeless, eternal truths that need to be connected to biblical Christian living. Hold all of James in your mind and in your teaching as you consider each part and explore the biblical fullness of this wonderful book. It will lead to Christian maturity and sound Biblical exploration and thinking.

4. Real world faith: Application is always a key in good teaching. Lead your hearers to do critical thinking about how we can apply James' teaching about dealing with trials and temptations, practicing wisdom, money, considering and caring for others based on looks, and taking care of the poor and the widow in the world they are living in now. One need not look far or even beyond their own lives and community to find such opportunities for thoughtful application of the Scriptures. Do that work.

Remember to pray as you go. Teach the Word as it stands and let God do the gracious work of leading believers through His Word to living the holy life.

STEVEN HOSKINS is associate professor of Religion at Trevecca Nazarene University. His an ordained elder in the Church of the Nazarene, the Promotional Secretary of the Wesleyan Theological Society, and founder of the Wesleyan Historical Society.

The Message of James

SESSION 7

Session Outcome

To acknowledge that Christlike living results from hearts and minds illuminated by the word of truth.

Customize:

Spirit is the password to access expanded teaching helps on FoundryLeader.com.

Discover:

Illustrated Bible Life looks at what James says about living the Christian life, and provides verse-by-verse commentary on the Scripture passage.

April

16

FAITH AND GOOD WORKS

The word of truth that gives us new life also guides us in living that new life.

THE WORD

JAMES 1:17-27

Every good and perfect gift is from above, coming down from the Father of the heavenly lights, who does not change like shifting shadows. [18]He chose to give us birth through the word of truth, that we might be a kind of firstfruits of all he created.

[19]My dear brothers and sisters, take note of this: Everyone should be quick to listen, slow to speak and slow to become angry, [20]because human anger does not produce the righteousness that God desires. [21]Therefore, get rid of all moral filth and the evil that is so prevalent and humbly accept the word planted in you, which can save you.

KEY VERSE **[22]Do not merely listen to the word, and so deceive yourselves. Do what it says.** [23]Anyone who listens to the word but does not do what it says is like someone who looks at his face in a mirror [24]and, after looking at himself, goes away and immediately forgets what he looks like. [25]But whoever looks intently into the perfect law that gives freedom, and continues in it—not forgetting what they have heard, but doing it—they will be blessed in what they do.

[26]Those who consider themselves religious and yet do not keep a tight rein on their tongues deceive themselves, and their religion is worthless. [27]Religion that God our Father accepts as pure and faultless is this: to look after orphans and widows in their distress and to keep oneself from being polluted by the world.

2:14-18

[14]What good is it, my brothers and sisters, if someone claims to have faith but has no deeds? Can such faith save them? [15]Suppose a brother or a sister is without clothes and daily food. [16]If one of you says to them, "Go in peace; keep warm and well fed," but does noth-

Last Week:

We gained a deeper understanding of the way the resurrection of Jesus means victory over death and life everlasting.

This Week:

We will gain a deeper understanding that there should be no separation between hearing and doing God's Word.

ing about their physical needs, what good is it? ¹⁷In the same way, faith by itself, if it is not accompanied by action, is dead.

¹⁸But someone will say, "You have faith; I have deeds."

Show me your faith without deeds, and I will show you my faith by my deeds.

ENGAGE THE WORD

THE GOD WHO LAVISHES LOVE

James 1:17-18

James begins this section of Scripture with a glorious truth (1:17): The fountain of goodness and grace is the God who lavishes His love on us. One implication of this verse is that wherever we see good around the world, God's fingerprints are evident. James is writing to people who are enduring trials. He is counteracting the idea that God is the source of the temptations. Rather than tempting us, God paves the path toward success in every moment of decision.

James indicates that God's character never changes. We grow up expecting that people change. James reminds his readers that God "does not change like shifting shadows" (1:17b). The character of God reminds us that He will always be faithful. James also points out that, "He chose to give us birth through the word of truth, that we might be a kind of firstfruits of all he created" (1:18). God renews us in the midst of life "through the word of truth" and intends us to be evidence of His goodness and grace (see **Did You Know?**).

LISTEN!

James 1:19-21

James begins this passage with startling language, "Take note." So the gravity of this message is not missed, the reader is reminded that it matters that we listen. The message is clear: God's people are eager to listen and slow to speak. It is easy to be planning the response to a comment before it is finished. However, people who are born by the word of truth are humble, and listening to others is an act of humble faith and respect. When we listen, we live out the truth that the

Notes:

_____

_____

_____

_____

_____

_____

_____

_____

_____

_____

_____

_____

_____

_____

_____

_____

▶ **Watch:**

Dr. Roger Hahn introduces this unit on James.

🔊 **Listen:**

FoundryLeader.com: This week's *Illustrated Bible Life* "Article Out Loud" examines James' words about the need for action as well as words when it comes to living out our faith.

Notes:

_____

_____

_____

_____

_____

_____

_____

_____

_____

_____

_____

_____

_____

_____

_____

_____

_____

Did You Know?

We understand the "word of truth" as the gospel message (Ephesians 1:13; Colossians 1:5; 2 Timothy 2:15). We encounter the good news of the gospel, respond to it, and apply its message to our lives. This is God's free gift offered to us and we reap its benefits when we willingly accept it.

DOERS OF THE WORD

person speaking is made in the image of God. The longer I follow God and His Word, the more I make sure I fully understand a person before I respond.

James calls his readers to see that we should not only be slow to speak but also slow to anger. Such an emotion reflects fear more than strength. Anger spills out of a heart that is lost and anxious in the midst of discussion. A heart born by the word of truth does not need to be defensive or abrasive. James reminds the reader that "human anger does not produce the righteousness that God desires" (1:20). The word of truth has nothing to do with the weakness denoted with anger. Sordidness and wickedness accompany anger, according to James. Therefore, he counsels his readers to greet anger with meekness. Such a response may seem counter-intuitive, but the implanted word of truth has the power to transform anger into grace.

James 1:22-25

The heart of the passage comes clearly into focus in this section. God calls all who profess His name to be doers of the Word. Doing is an active word, and hearing is more passive. A key word needs to be unpacked here: deception. Those that merely listen are deceiving themselves, according to James. Such people hear but quickly forget. It is as if they look in the mirror with no more depth than a casual glance. They look but do not really see. Whether they are pleased or disquieted, the message dies moments later. It means little and ends up nowhere. James adds, "But whoever looks intently into the perfect law that gives freedom, and continues in it—not forgetting what they have heard, but doing it—they will be blessed in what they do" (1:25). Jesus calls individuals to drop their nets and follow Him immediately. He is not interested in those that assign anything of higher priority than the call to follow. When we see ourselves in the light of the perfect law, freedom comes into focus.

Discover:

Religious life that God finds genuine is not simply a matter of words or prayers voiced, nor is it a matter of beliefs confessed. Rather, the religion that God accepts as "pure and faultless" concerns both speech and action. Find out what James has to say about this important topic in this week's *Illustrated Bible Life* article, "James and the Christian Life."

Notes:

Think About It

The Greek language has several words for anger. One of those words means a sudden burst of emotional anger arising from frustration. Another word means something like indignation, the word used for anger in this passage. It also means a deep and persistent rage. This word can refer to God's wrath toward sin. When James uses this in relation to human beings, it means selfish resentment. The anger that is inconsistent with righteousness is this self-centered resistance to God's truth.

CONTROL THE TONGUE
James 1:26-27

James extends his argument in verses 26-27 when he links religion with our speech. Those who follow Jesus must get control of their tongues. Words have the power to bless and to curse. James reminds his readers that we render religion worthless when we reject the will of God to transform our thoughts and words. For those who are earnestly seeking to serve God, faith is not merely an internal possession, but a passion to care for others and live a pure life.

FAITH AND ACTION
James 2:14-18

James connects faith and action, "What good is it, my brothers and sisters, if someone claims to have faith but has no deeds? Can such faith save them?" (2:14). Later, he writes, "In the same way, faith by itself, if it is not accompanied by action, is dead" (2:17). This calls to mind the material flow between grace and character. Grace is not a cloak that hides our sin from God for the sake of Christ. Some might describe this as an alien righteousness precariously resting upon us. The Wesleyan-Holiness tradition joins the best lights of the Christian tradition to embrace transformational righteousness. We are changed from the inside out. We are not saved to continue in sin. Rather, we are healed of sin's diseases. In light of our spiritual transformation, our actions (deeds) become an expression of our faith.

REFLECT In what ways can you be a doer of the Word this week?

HENRY SPAULDING, II is president of Mount Vernon Nazarene University, Mount Vernon, Ohio.

Discussion Guide

Connect to My Experience

Begin by asking your group:.

- Have you ever been bored or distracted when someone was speaking? If so, what caused this disconnect?

- What are the characteristics of a bad listener? What are the characteristics of a good listener?

Transition:

In this session, we will learn how to be deliberate listeners who become doers of God's Word because we focus on God's character first.

Connect to the Word

Invite someone to read James 1:17-18 and consider the following,

To be good listeners, it is important to know who is speaking and why. It is especially true when we want to cultivate good listening habits as we read or hear the Word of God.

- How does James characterize who God is in verses 17-18?

- What is the connection between God's good gifts and His character?

- What does it mean that God "does not change like shifting shadows"? Why is this an important truth as it relates to God's Word?

- How are we the "firstfruits" of God? (See **Insight**.)

Invite someone to read James 1:19-21 and consider the following,

In these verses, James shares traits of a growing and mature Christian.

- According to James, what is the relationship between speaking, listening, and anger? (v. 19)

- What does anger have to do with righteousness? (The anger in this case is uncontrolled, thoughtless, and hurtful. It is inconsistent with Christlikeness.)

- What are healthy ways people can deal with anger? How are the actions James suggests a good antidote for anger problems?

- What are the characteristics of someone who wants to listen and obey God's Word?

- What is involved in being quick to listen and slow to speak?

Too many times we double the use of our mouth and reduce the use of our ears.

- What contaminates our listening and speaking according to verse 21?

- In what ways can God's Word be planted in us? (studying and obeying)

Invite someone to read James 1:22-25 and consider the following,

James shares a revealing metaphor in his desire to make a strong connection between listening to God's Word and obeying it.

- What did James mean when he cautioned them not to deceive themselves? (Casual listening leads to a lack of knowledge about God and God's Word [see Colossians 2:4]. We must seek understanding by listening and doing.)

- How is God's Word our mirror?

- According to verse 25, how does James want us treat God's Word when we listen to it?

Insight

Firstfruits is a harvest term referring to the first and best produce or the first born among animals and humans. God wants the first of everything, not because He is greedy but because we tend to be hoarders. When we give ourselves to God, we become forerunners of the great harvest God wants to bring in before the end of the world.

How does focused attention and intention toward God's Word bring freedom?

Read James 1:22 again. What is the benefit of listening to God's Word?

Invite someone to read James 1:26-27 and consider the following,

Now James gets specific.

What is the meaning of being religious in today's culture?

According to verse 26-27, what is a pure and faultless religion?

Why should believers maintain good control over what they say? (v. 26).

What does it mean to "keep oneself from being polluted by the world"? (v. 27)

Invite someone to read James 2:14-18 and consider the following,

James reminds us that listening to God's Word always gives us something to obey.

How do faith and works go together in the life of a follower of Christ?

In what way does faith die without action?

Just because we do good things for others, does that mean we do them because of our faith? Why or why not?

James reminds us that there is a spiritual growth factor at work between faith and action.

What good is faith without deeds?

Is faith without an others-oriented perspective enough by God's standards?

If we do nothing about someone's physical needs, how does it affect his/her ability to listen to spiritual truth?

What causes dead faith?

In what ways does faith in action speak without words?

Connect to My Life and the World

Consider how you can put the Word into practice this week using any of the following ideas:

Make a gratitude list. What gifts have you taken for granted? How can you "pay it forward" and do something for someone because of what God has done for you?

Read today's scripture passages over again this week. Let it be your mirror. Where are you reflecting what God's Word tells you to do? How will you address what God helps you to see?

Consider a faith-works project for your group. Take a love-basket to someone who needs encouragement. Adopt a homebound senior who could use some help at their home. Find a mission project in your community where you can be a hands-on contributor.

Close in prayer.

Sessions 7-11 are written by Gay Leonard

Gay is a writer, editorial consultant, and author/compiler of five books, including *Articles of Faith: What Nazarenes Believe and Why*. She has spent a lifetime of ministry with her husband, Larry.

The Message of James

Session Outcome

To understand that the objective of every believer and Christian community must be impartiality, openness, and a generous equality at every level.

Customize:

Spirit is the password to access expanded teaching helps on FoundryLeader.com.

Discover:

Illustrated Bible Life looks at class and economic differences in the first century, and provides verse-by-verse commentary on the Scripture passage.

April

23

THE PROBLEM WITH PARTIALITY

Christians are not to show favoritism.

THE WORD

JAMES 2:1-13

My brothers and sisters, believers in our glorious Lord Jesus Christ must not show favoritism. ²Suppose a man comes into your meeting wearing a gold ring and fine clothes, and a poor man in filthy old clothes also comes in. ³If you show special attention to the man wearing fine clothes and say, "Here's a good seat for you," but say to the poor man, "You stand there" or "Sit on the floor by my feet," ⁴have you not discriminated among yourselves and become judges with evil thoughts?

⁵Listen, my dear brothers and sisters: Has not God chosen those who are poor in the eyes of the world to be rich in faith and to inherit the kingdom he promised those who love him? ⁶But you have dishonored the poor. Is it not the rich who are exploiting you? Are they not the ones who are dragging you into court? ⁷Are they not the ones who are blaspheming the noble name of him to whom you belong?

KEY VERSES

⁸If you really keep the royal law found in Scripture, "Love your neighbor as yourself," you are doing right. ⁹But if you show favoritism, you sin and are convicted by the law as lawbreakers. ¹⁰For whoever keeps the whole law and yet stumbles at just one point is guilty of breaking all of it. ¹¹For he who said, "You shall not commit adultery," also said, "You shall not murder." If you do not commit adultery but do commit murder, you have become a lawbreaker.

¹²Speak and act as those who are going to be judged by the law that gives freedom, ¹³because judgment without mercy will be shown to anyone who has not been merciful. Mercy triumphs over judgment.

Last Week:

We explored the way believers affirm their faith through good works.

This Week:

We will explore the way that showing favoritism is inconsistent with the teachings of Christ.

Notes:

_____

_____

_____

_____

_____

_____

_____

_____

_____

_____

_____

_____

_____

_____

_____

_____

_____

_____

_____

Session 8

ENGAGE THE WORD

Loving God and neighbor expresses a profound truth regarding faith. Last week we noted that grace renders us responsible for reflecting the great gift of salvation to others. God's gift to us becomes a gift to those who cross our path. This week, we will look at another significant passage of scripture in our attempt to understand our Christian faith and practice.

James seeks to address the implications that flow from faith in "our glorious Lord" (2:1b). This move further affirms that our faith puts us to work; it is an active faith. Faith is an enfleshed intention to accept the gift of salvation and extend the same gift to those who are hungry or thirsty, both spiritually and physically. When Jesus walked the earth, He touched the untouchable and marginalized. He recognized men and women that society ignored. The message of James in this passage gestures toward an authentic faith expressed through inclusive grace. The first service held by Phineas Bresee, the founding personality of the Church of the Nazarene, was in a rescue mission. Working on behalf of the poor embodies a vital faith as well as holiness theology.

FAVORITISM INCONSISTENT WITH FAITH

James 2:1-7

James affirms in this great passage that favoritism is inconsistent with a vital faith. He writes, "My brothers and sisters, believers in our glorious Lord Jesus Christ must not show favoritism" (2:1). This reveals a deep disconnect among those in the church between their faith and life. Wesley often asked, "How is it with your soul today?" to members of his small groups. We also understand that faith is not merely an abstract intention to believe. Rather, it is a strong commitment to being what we believe. Gold rings and fine clothes should never translate to priority in the church. This practice of preference based on status in life is repugnant to James and contradictory to the gospel.

🔊 **Listen:**

FoundryLeader.com: This week's *Illustrated Bible Life* "Article Out Loud" examines what life was like for rich and poor in the days of the early church.

Notes:

_____

_____

_____

_____

_____

_____

_____

_____

_____

_____

_____

_____

_____

_____

_____

_____

_____

Did You Know?

James had good reason to question the rich (2:6). In Israel and throughout the Roman Empire, the rich were exploiting the poor. Roman society was divided into classes, and the higher classes had a favored status throughout the empire. In fact, Roman laws favored the rich and penalties prescribed by the laws were tougher on the lower class.

James further states: "Listen, my dear brothers and sisters: Has not God chosen those who are poor in the eyes of the world to be rich in faith and to inherit the kingdom he promised those who love him?" (2:5). This does not exalt poverty in any way; however, it does recognize that God often finds the poor more receptive. Fine clothes in and of themselves do not bar a person from the kingdom. Admittance into the kingdom comes to those who, in true repentance, humble themselves at the cross, whatever the social class. Jesus was born in a manger to a poor family. He understood at eye level hunger and sickness. Those who lavish themselves with unnecessary things might find it more difficult to understand the plight of the poor and thereby miss the good news of the gospel. When the privileged in life wield power at the expense of the poor, they dishonor God.

Wesley was systematically driven away from every parish in the Church of England because he attracted the margins of society to his services which made the wealthy uncomfortable. Because of this, he began preaching in the field with great success. While God can use anyone no matter their social and economic status, the more receptive group is often the poor. It is important to note that just as it is essential for the rich not to exclude the poor, the poor must not assume priority over the rich. It is always a matter of a receptive heart.

LAW AND LOVE

James 2:8-13

The fascination with the law by the Pharisees did not exclude them from the ultimate law of love. James writes, "If you really keep the royal law found in Scripture, 'Love your neighbor as yourself,' you are doing right. But if you show favoritism, you sin and are convicted by the law as lawbreakers" (2:8-9). The insight shared here reaches to the intention of the law itself. It is just as wrong to juxtapose law and love because love is both the genesis and fulfillment of the

Discover:

The widening gap of economic differences is one of the most worrying issues of societies. This is not new, but an age-old problem. How did the church in the first century navigate this issue? This week's *Illustrated Bible Life* article, "Class and Economy in the First Century," explains.

Think About It
What happens when Christians act out their faith in deeds of goodness just as their Master did? The result is a heart filled with that merciful spirit that will act with compassion.

law. When we love our neighbor, we catch the spirit of the law itself. An essential unity emerges here. James writes, "Speak and act as those who are going to be judged by the law that gives freedom, because judgment without mercy will be shown to anyone who has not been merciful. Mercy triumphs over judgment" (2:10-13). Ultimately, loving our neighbor opens our life to Spirit-engendered liberty. We become what God intends when we truly love our neighbor in worship of God. It opens up the mercy of God for us. God lavishes His love upon us, and until we extend that same mercy to our neighbor, we do not fully understand it.

This passage of scripture raises a significant insight into the Christian faith. This insight underwrites what we talked about last week in that grace calls us to a responsible life. Here the same point is made by affirming that partiality based on social status betrays our faith.

Wesley was a very well-educated person with an appointment at Oxford University. He had every reason to distance himself from the poverty and desperation of the common person. Yet, he pursued them and served them until the very end of his life. Holiness refuses to surrender to an ethereal and abstract faith. Rather, a clear-headed assessment of sin joins with a sense of the power of grace. The division and strife of our world would be immensely and positively transformed by a vision of our equal status at the foot of the cross.

REFLECT How might showing no favoritism or preference in our relationships witness to the power of the Christian faith?

HENRY SPAULDING, II

Notes:

_____

_____

_____

_____

_____

_____

_____

_____

_____

_____

_____

_____

_____

_____

_____

_____

Discussion Guide

 Connect to My Experience

Discrimination and prejudice are words we hear a lot in the media today. James uses another word to talk about this divisive practice. He calls it favoritism. No matter what word you use, the result is negative.

- Have you ever experienced or witnessed discrimination?
- How did it make you feel?
- Why do you think people show favoritism?

Transition:

Today James teaches how our natural bent toward unexamined perceptions and self-centered thinking is at odds with what Jesus practiced and taught.

Connect to the Word

Invite someone to read James 2:1-7, then discuss the following,

James takes a blunt approach to discrimination. Like Jesus, he gave them a picture of what favoritism looks like. Then, he makes them face the spiritual danger involved.

- How does James address his readers in verses 1 and 5? How does this help James communicate a sensitive message?
- What reason does James give for rejecting favoritism in verse 1?
- Who does favoritism really favor? Why?

Discrimination is a way to divide people into groups in ways that influence how we respond to them. It is based on perceptions, generalizations, and often ignorance.

- In verse 4, what role does James say we take on when we discriminate?
- In the illustration James uses, how did the people divide the guests?
- What if the two guests James described visited your group? What might your first thoughts be? Which person would you be comfortable to reach out to and why?
- What is often at the root of discrimination? (example: misunderstanding)

Jesus taught us not to judge or we will be judged by the same standards (Matthew 7:1).

- According to verse 7, why should we refuse to treat people in a lower economic category with less respect?
- What reason does James give in verses 6-7 for refusing to show favoritism just because someone has money?

The world gives us inadequate models for anti-discrimination. For Christians, Jesus is our model. He never discriminated and yet never ignored actions or attitudes that did not please God.

- What are some of the ways Jesus treated all people without discrimination?
- How could He refuse discrimination and still call people to repentance?
- How does Jesus' model help us intersect with people we don't know or understand?
- The session writer refers to "inclusive grace." How does God's inclusive grace create more similarities than differences to reject favoritism?

Invite someone to read James 2:8-13, then discuss the following,

James keeps getting more personal about this subject. In these verses he returns to making sure we know who the judge is, who will be judged, and how.

Insight

The believer in whom the royal law of love operates will have nothing to do with any action that separates or divides brothers and sisters in Christ. The church must constantly guard against the temptation to show preference on any level which divide people from one another.

- What is the "royal law" mentioned in verse 8? (The royal law is stated in in v. 8, "Love your neighbor as yourself." It is also found in Leviticus 19:18; Matthew 19:19; 22:39; Mark 12:31, 33; Luke 10:27; Romans 13:9; Galatians 5:14.)

- How should we let this "royal law" guide our treatment of all people? Share an example of the "royal law" in action you have seen or experienced.

- In verse 9, what does James call someone who shows favoritism? (Lawbreakers of the law of love.)

- How is breaking one commandment of God's law the same as breaking them all? (Sin is sin and effects our relationship with God. All sin must be confessed and repented of.)

When we don't love God with all our heart, soul, and mind, we are vulnerable to break other commandments. This vulnerability should help us lead with mercy in all our relationships.

- According to verses 12-13, how should we treat all people?

- If we judge others—show partiality and discriminate—how will we be judged?

- Does extending mercy mean we ignore sin? Why or why not?

- How does mercy "triumph over judgment"?

- How do we betray our faith by participating in attitudes and actions that discriminate?

Connect to My Life and the World

To apply James' warnings and teaching, we must be willing to check our impressions and actions by God's Word. Consider how these activities might give you a chance to practice impartiality.

- Share random acts of kindness to people who don't expect it.

- Consider a service activity that would place you with people who don't live like you.

- Think about a "good neighbor" project for your church.

- Consider a "good neighbor" project in your neighborhood.

End your session with this compilation of Scripture as your prayer for the week:

- My brothers and sisters, believers in our glorious Lord Jesus Christ must not show favoritism (James 2:1).

- Do not judge, or you too will be judged (Matthew 7:1).

- Love your neighbor as yourself (Matthew 22: 39).

- Therefore, as God's chosen people, holy and dearly loved, clothe yourselves with compassion, kindness, humility, gentleness and patience. . . . and over all these virtues put on love (Colossians 3:12, 14a).

- Have the same mindset as Christ Jesus (Philippians 2:5b).

Dismiss the group to serve their world without favoritism and with the love God empowers.

Unit 2
The Message of James

Session Outcome

To accept personal accountability for speech control, with God's help.

Customize:

Spirit is the password to access expanded teaching helps on FoundryLeader.com.

Discover:

Illustrated Bible Life takes a look at the power of words, especially in ancient times, and provides verse-by-verse commentary on the Scripture passage.

April
30

FAITH AND GOOD WORDS

Our speech needs to be brought under the control of Christ.

THE WORD

JAMES 3:1-12

Not many of you should become teachers, my fellow believers, because you know that we who teach will be judged more strictly. ²We all stumble in many ways. Anyone who is never at fault in what they say is perfect, able to keep their whole body in check.

³When we put bits into the mouths of horses to make them obey us, we can turn the whole animal. ⁴Or take ships as an example. Although they are so large and are driven by strong winds, they are steered by a very small rudder wherever the pilot wants to go. ⁵Likewise, the tongue is a small part of the body, but it makes great boasts. Consider what a great forest is set on fire by a small spark. ⁶The tongue also is a fire, a world of evil among the parts of the body. It corrupts the whole body, sets the whole course of one's life on fire, and is itself set on fire by hell.

⁷All kinds of animals, birds, reptiles and sea creatures are being tamed and have been tamed by mankind, ⁸but no human being can tame the tongue. It is a restless evil, full of deadly poison.

KEY VERSES **⁹With the tongue we praise our Lord and Father, and with it we curse human beings, who have been made in God's likeness. ¹⁰Out of the same mouth come praise and cursing. My brothers and sisters, this should not be.** ¹¹Can both fresh water and salt water flow from the same spring? ¹²My brothers and sisters, can a fig tree bear olives, or a grapevine bear figs? Neither can a salt spring produce fresh water.

17-18 ¹⁷But the wisdom that comes from heaven is first of all pure; then peace-loving, considerate, submissive, full of mercy and good

Last Week:

We saw that we must never permit discrimination that separates, rips, or tears at the fabric of the body of Christ.

This Week:

We will see the importance of bringing our speech under the control of Christ.

Session 9

fruit, impartial and sincere. ¹⁸Peacemakers who sow in peace reap a harvest of righteousness.

ENGAGE THE WORD

God blesses us with minds and, for the most part, the capacity to speak. James is aware that our ability to speak is a powerful gift that can become a blessing or a curse.

TEACHERS

James 3:1-5

James begins with a stark warning, "Not many of you should become teachers, my fellow believers, because you know that we who teach will be judged more strictly" (v. 1). I can remember the words of my professors over the years. Their voices echo in my mind as I reflect on the issues presented to me. Even as I embrace another conclusion occasionally, the voices remain. Teachers are a gift, but they carry a special burden to be careful in the way they use their voice. It is a good reminder of the serious responsibility and accountability placed upon those who teach.

James continues his exhortation, "We all stumble in many ways. Anyone who is never at fault in what they say is perfect, able to keep their whole body in check" (v. 2). This is a powerful image. We all make mistakes, and the place where we are most likely to make a mistake is in speech. Many times, a word slips out before we know it. James uses strong metaphors to get at the issue. He refers to "bits into the mouths of horses" and "rudders" for a ship. The idea seems to be that small parts control large objects (i.e., horses and ships). He closes the paragraph with a clear conclusion, "Likewise, the tongue is a small part of the body, but it makes great boasts. Consider what a great forest is set on fire by a small spark" (v. 5). If we are not careful, our words have a way of controlling our lives. Therefore, discipline is required not only of those who teach, but anyone who seeks to embody holiness.

🔊 **Listen:**

FoundryLeader.com: The power of the spoken word is the topic of this week's *Illustrated Bible Life* "Article Out Loud."

Notes:

_____

_____

_____

_____

_____

_____

_____

_____

_____

_____

_____

_____

_____

_____

_____

Did You Know?

The use of the word "hell" in 3:6b underscores a vivid image in the mind of those who read this book. It refers immediately to a ditch or valley outside the city walls where garbage burned. Because it continually burned, the smoke served as a reminder of judgment. The association made by James provides a visible image of the uncontrolled tongue.

DANGER AND BLESSING OF SPEECH

WISDOM FROM ABOVE

James 3:6-12

The message of this passage builds strong support for the danger and the blessing of speech. Our words can start wars, but they also can bring peace. James offers a bleak view of the tongue, "The tongue also is a fire, a world of evil among the parts of the body. It corrupts the whole body, sets the whole course of one's life on fire, and is itself set on fire by hell" (v. 6). It is exceedingly difficult to tame the tongue. James refers to the tongue as "a restless evil, full of deadly poison" (3:8b). My mother often told me that sticks and stones may break my bones, but words will never hurt me. This was conventional wisdom, but I have found that bones often heal before the bruises on our soul caused by words. Of course, there is a deeper message contained here.

The doctrinal and moral convictions of the Christian faith are treasures for those who follow Christ. Understanding requires maturity in the face of all the temptations to speak or act precipitously. James adds, "With the tongue we praise our Lord and Father, and with it we curse human beings, who have been made in God's likeness. Out of the same mouth come praise and cursing. My brothers and sisters, this should not be" (vv. 9-10). Can falsehood and division emerge from a heart made new in Christ? How likely is it for brackish to emerge from freshwater? Can a fig tree yield olives or a grapevine figs? The answer is obvious, no! Words matter because they are an outside revelation of the inside condition of the heart.

James 3:17-18

The full impact of this passage comes into focus at the end of the chapter. James writes, "But the wisdom that comes from heaven is first of all pure; then peace-loving, considerate, submissive, full of mercy and good fruit, impartial and sincere" (v. 17). This is in complete contrast to boastful earthly, unspiritual, and devilish ambitions. This brings our minds back

Discover:

Today's culture often seems to advocate against telling the truth— or the truth in its fullness. We are encouraged to shade the truth to put ourselves in the best light. In the biblical world, however, the spoken and written word was treated with much greater respect. Find out more about the ancient world's regard for words in this week's *Illustrated Bible Life* article, "The Value of the Spoken Word."

Notes:

Think About It

The church needs people who love God and others; who will avoid petty quarreling and slander; who can control their speech; and who will seek God's wisdom so that the church can partake of the harvest of righteousness and peace.

around to speech. These verses are reminiscent of the passage in Galatians where Paul contrasts the fruit of the Spirit with works of the flesh. We talk about exercising wisdom a good deal in the church. If we are not careful, these times can be fraught with the temptation to set the forest ablaze (v. 5). However, when our minds embrace the wisdom from above, our words will reflect "a harvest of righteousness."

John Wesley writes, "And the principle productive of this righteousness is sown, like good seed, in the peace of a believer's mind, and brings forth a plentiful harvest of happiness (which is the proper fruit of righteousness) for them that make peace—That labour to promote this pure and holy peace among (humankind)" (*Explanatory Notes on the New Testament*, 865).

The Wesleyan-Holiness tradition finds its passion in the way grace heals sin's diseases. We understand that all who follow find forgiveness in Christ by faith through grace for our transgressions. All theological traditions understand the importance of living a redeemed life, but the Wesleyan-Holiness tradition provides a faithful path by which to address these doctrinal convictions so we might address character. This is a theology of transformation.

James concludes with a wonderful description of wisdom from above and disciplined speech, "But the wisdom that comes from heaven is first of all pure; then peace-loving, considerate, submissive, full of mercy and good fruit, impartial and sincere. Peacemakers who sow in peace reap a harvest of righteousness" (vv. 17-18). This is because wisdom from above calls us to reflect on our citizenship in another kingdom.

REFLECT How do our words bless or condemn others? How does our speech embody wisdom?

HENRY SPAULDING, II

Discussion Guide

 Connect to My Experience

Ask the group to consider a time when they knew they said the wrong thing or said it in a way that caused hurt. Consider these questions:

- When did you know it was problematic?
- How did you recognize it as a problem?
- What did you do about it and why?

Transition:

Words carry more power to hurt than we recognize. This week's session delves into James' reminder of the accountability God requires as we use our words.

Connect to the Word

Invite someone to read James 3:1-5a, then consider the following,

Words are so much a part of our daily lives that we don't think about them as much as we should. James gives us warnings and illustrations to help us become word-wise.

- Why do you think James starts with a warning to teachers?
- Why do you think teachers are judged "more strictly"? (The teacher is more accountable because of his/her greater influence, and because he/she instructs others how to live.)
- Besides the people who teach by profession, or those in ministry, who else should we include in this group of teachers? (parents, leaders)
- The church seems to demand a higher standard of conduct from its leaders—pastors, church board members, teachers-—than it does the average member. Is this fair? Why or why not?
- How would you interpret verse 2? Is anyone ever perfect? (Perfect here means mature. Self-restraint empowered by the Holy Spirit.)

James illustrates the importance of directing our words in positive ways with two examples: a horse's bit and a boat's rudder.

- What is the purpose of a horse's bit is and how does it aid the rider?
- How does James compare the tongue and the words it forms with a bit?
- How does a rudder work? What happens if you don't have a rudder or it doesn't work properly?
- How does James compare the tongue and the words it forms to a rudder?
- James says, "The tongue is a small part of the body, but it makes great boasts." What do you think he means by this statement? (It is small, but has power.)

Invite someone to read James 3:5b-12, then consider the following,

James turns to the way a small spark can cause a huge fire.

- How can our words do the same damage as a tiny spark? What examples of this have you seen?
- Why does James indicate it is easier to tame wildlife than our tongues? Do you agree or disagree? Explain.

He is pushing us to be responsible and discerning before we speak. He wants us to confront the good, the bad, and the poisonous use of words.

- What is an example of a restless or evil tongue?

Insight

Logos is used in the New Testament Greek language for "word." Logos has a layered meaning that goes past letters and syllables to embody message. When John called Jesus "the Word," he reached back to creation when God's word created our world. James calls us to use our words for creative possibilities, too.

■ Where do people today practice a restless tongue the most?

James turns to a picture of how our communication should use words in God-pleasing ways in verses 9-12. The most important of those ways is to praise God.

■ How do our negative words keep us from reflecting God's image?

■ What does a freshwater spring teach us according to verse 11? (A spring cannot produce both fresh and salt water. We must allow God to produce in us pure water/speech. They cannot coexist.)

■ How does an olive tree or grapevine remind us of what should come from our mouths? (We are to produce the fruit of godly character—the fruit of righteousness [3:18].)

■ What did God create our mouths/tongues/speech to do?

■ If God promises to help keep our words beneficial, why do we have so much trouble taming our tongues?

Invite someone to read James 3:17-18, then consider the following,

James points us to the truth that true wisdom is God-sourced wisdom.

■ Name the qualities of wisdom from heaven. (Consider making a list on a whiteboard of the words James uses to describe the wisdom that tames our speech.)

■ Ask the group to define each quality and share examples of each. (Example: Peace-loving: the emphasis is on peaceful relationships between persons.)

■ What is the goal of wise words according to verse 18?

■ What does it mean to "sow peace" and to "reap a harvest of righteousness"?

Connect to My Life and the World

People today like to say what they think. Many speak their mind regardless of the damage their words might do.

■ How should our speech be different when it is under the control of the Holy Spirit?

■ What are some ways we could improve our speech and bring it under the control of the Holy Spirit? (avoid negative speech, wait before responding to criticism, focus on positive things, pause before speaking)

Perhaps the best medicine to treat a restless or untamed tongue is to read what Proverbs says about our words.

—Take hold of my words with all your heart (Proverbs 4:4).

—Keep my words and store up my commands within you (Proverbs 7:1).

—The prudent hold their tongues (Proverbs 10:19b).

—The words of the reckless pierce like swords, but the tongue of the wise brings healing (Proverbs 12:18).

—Gracious words are a honeycomb, sweet to the soul and healing to the bones (Proverbs 16:24).

—The one who has knowledge uses words with restraint (Proverbs 17:27a).

Close with prayer.

SESSION 10

Session Outcome

To affirm that we must strive, with God's help, to do the good that we can do.

Customize:

Spirit is the password to access expanded teaching helps on FoundryLeader.com.

Discover:

Illustrated Bible Life explores the topic of judgment of others, and gives verse-by-verse commentary on the Scripture passage.

May

7

FAITH AND GOD'S PROVIDENCE

God's providential blessings thrive in our lives when we are engaged in good works that honor both God's mission as well as God's character.

THE WORD

JAMES 4:4-17

You adulterous people, don't you know that friendship with the world means enmity against God? Therefore, anyone who chooses to be a friend of the world becomes an enemy of God. ⁵Or do you think Scripture says without reason that he jealously longs for the spirit he has caused to dwell in us? ⁶But he gives us more grace. That is why Scripture says: "God opposes the proud but shows favor to the humble."

⁷Submit yourselves, then, to God. Resist the devil, and he will flee from you. ⁸Come near to God and he will come near to you. Wash your hands, you sinners, and purify your hearts, you double-minded. ⁹Grieve, mourn and wail. Change your laughter to mourning and your joy to gloom. ¹⁰Humble yourselves before the Lord, and he will lift you up.

¹¹Brothers and sisters, do not slander one another. Anyone who speaks against a brother or sister or judges them speaks against the law and judges it. When you judge the law, you are not keeping it, but sitting in judgment on it. ¹²There is only one Lawgiver and Judge, the one who is able to save and destroy. But you—who are you to judge your neighbor?

¹³Now listen, you who say, "Today or tomorrow we will go to this or that city, spend a year there, carry on business and make money." ¹⁴Why, you do not even know what will happen tomorrow. What is your life? You are a mist that appears for a little while and then vanishes. **KEY VERSE** ¹⁵**Instead, you ought to say, "If it is the Lord's will, we will live and do this or that."** ¹⁶As it is, you boast in your arrogant schemes. All such boasting is evil. ¹⁷If anyone, then, knows the good they ought to do and doesn't do it, it is sin for them.

Last Week:

We recognized that controlling the tongue requires, with God's help, diligent discipline.

This Week:

We will recognize that Christians thrive in God's providential resources when engaged in the mission and work of God.

Session 10

ENGAGE THE WORD

God calls us and enables us for a new life in Christ. With Jesus, we are able to live a different and better life. The prevailing theme of Christian faith is that submission to God opens up a completely new world to us.

DESIRES INTO VIRTUES

James 4:4-12

The first verses of chapter 4 frame the words of this passage. James begins his analysis by examining desire (4:1). James chooses "desires" (or cravings) to express his astonishment. It is an extreme term that connotes an irrational need. It is highly important that James suggests that these cravings are at the root of conflicts and disputes. James goes on to write, "You desire but do not have, so you kill. You covet but you cannot get what you want, so you quarrel and fight. You do not have because you do not ask God" (4:2). He means to convey that once our desires become cravings, they can take us to a place we never imagined.

James asks a penetrating question, "You adulterous people, don't you know that friendship with the world means enmity against God? Therefore, anyone who chooses to be a friend of the world becomes an enemy of God" (4:4). The world constantly seeks to shape our lives and push us into its mold. This happens through words, images, and ideas. It may seem "natural" for many to find the allure of the secular compelling, but it is a wide path that leads to destruction.

James writes, "Or do you think Scripture says without reason that he jealously longs for the spirit he has caused to dwell in us" (4:5)? These worldy voices screaming at us only get our attention when we forget the depth of God's love for us. The promise comes through clearly, "But he gives us more grace. That is why Scripture says: 'God opposes the proud but shows favor to the humble'" (4:6). There is grace sufficient to conquer the pull of the world in our life. James' answer rings through the ages, "Submit yourselves, then, to

🔊 **Listen:**

FoundryLeader.com: This week's *Illustrated Bible Life* "Article Out Loud" examines what two key passages in the New Testament tell us about judging others.

Notes:

_____

_____

_____

_____

_____

_____

_____

_____

_____

_____

_____

_____

_____

_____

_____

_____

_____

_____

Did You Know?

The expression "double-minded" or "double-souled" might be illuminated by thinking in terms of synonymous parallelism. Therefore, it opens a way to understand sin as the futile attempt to satisfy both the world and God.

God" (4:7a). God provides the resources we need to avoid evil and embrace good. This is the joy of the gospel. It is holiness in succinct form—submit to God.

Fundamentally, evil is a lack not only of good but also of God. Because evil desires drain life from the world, resistance is both advisable and essential for wholeness. James writes, "Humble yourselves before the Lord, and he will lift you up" (4:10). God provides the remedy for our cravings by cleansing and purifying our hearts. Our Heavenly Father reorients our desires toward something that fulfills and heals sin's diseases.

Judgment is especially destructive when it arises from disoriented desires. We all make judgments every day. I make a judgment when pulling out into traffic. How fast is the car traveling? The traffic signal turns yellow. Can I get through the intersection before the light turns red? Or when reading, I determine the strength of the argument and the persuasiveness of the conclusion the author makes. James writes, "Brothers and sisters, do not slander one another. Anyone who speaks against a brother or sister or judges them speaks against the law and judges it. When you judge the law, you are not keeping it, but sitting in judgment on it" (4:11). This presents an intriguing observation. Those who judge assume a position above the law. James reminds his readers that assuming such a position makes us pretend to be lawgivers. Making sweeping pronouncements places us in a place where we do not belong. When our desires are undisciplined, we tend to judge and dismiss others. When we judge our neighbor, we cannot love them. When we submit to God, we understand that God alone is in a position to render judgment because God is sovereign.

SANCTIFIED LOVE   **James 4:13-17**

This entire section of Scripture explores the meaning of sanctified love. Thomas Aquinas defines love

Discover:

The Greek word translated "judge" appears more than 100 times in the New Testament. It has both negative and positive connotations, which means we need to weigh carefully how it is being used to understand what it means for us. To help us better understand this concept, we'll look at two key passages in this week's *Illustrated Bible Life* article, "Do Not Judge!"

Think About It

When we submit to God in humility, our hands become the hands of Christ, untainted by selfish motivation; our hearts become pure because they are no longer divided between the law of love and the law of self.

as willing the good for the other. God wills the good for all creation. The drama of salvation displays the passion that God has for humankind. We express our submission to God by the way we think about the future. James writes, "Now listen, you who say, 'Today or tomorrow we will go to this or that city, spend a year there, carry on business and make money.' Why, you do not even know what will happen tomorrow. What is your life? You are a mist that appears for a little while and then vanishes" (4:13-14). The ultimate act of craving is to think that the future is purely up to me. "My truth/way" can suggest a level of autonomy that upon reflection is foolish. We are not a choice or even a series of choices. Our life is a continuous reception of God's gift of love. This orients us to the future with a settled peace that the One who loves us most is guiding us. The sort of life defined by submission begins to understand that our desires should be conformed to the ever-new grace of God. Instead of "I will do such and such," we learn to say, "If God wills it, I will do such and such."

The Wesleyan-Holiness tradition affirms that God can direct our desires to the point that the power of sin is subverted. We do not need to live from one craving to another. Our freedom does not need to become bondage. God in Jesus Christ, through the power of the Holy Spirit, helps us conquer the unruly desires of life.

REFLECT How does a firm belief in the providential care of God enable us to embrace the stress and challenges of life with hope?

HENRY SPAULDING, II

Notes:

Discussion Guide

 Connect to My Experience

Think about how we know when we are living a life that pleases God. John Wesley gave us insight with his famous quote:

> "Do all the good you can,
> By all the means you can,
> In all the ways you can,
> In all the places you can,
> At all the times you can,
> To all the people you can,
> As long as ever you can."
> —John Wesley

- Can you do good but fail to please God? Why or why not?

- How do these actions influence daily choices?

Transition:

James is going to help us find clarity to the importance of doing good things as a response to God's invitation to live a life that pleases Him.

 **Connect to the Word**

Invite someone to read James 4:4-12, then discuss the following,

James begins chapter 4 with the real reason behind fights and quarrels. He identifies the problem as misplaced allegiance and calls it friendship with the world.

- How does James identify people who prioritize friendship with the world over friendship with God in verse 4?

- In what ways does friendship with the world affect our relationship with God?

- What are examples of friendship with the world that ignore God's standards?

- In what ways does the world try to shape our lives? How do we resist the world's influence?

- Enemy is a strong word. Why does friendship with the world make us an enemy of God?

James reminds them and us that God reaches out through grace to encourage us to return to His priorities and perspectives.

- How would you define grace?

- How do we receive God's grace?

- Why does God oppose the proud? (Pride makes us self-centered and keeps us from seeing our need for forgiveness. It prevents us from being humble.)

- Why does God show "favor to the humble"?

Ask someone to reread verses 7-10 slowly enough to give the group time to identify each action. Make a list on a whiteboard. Then answer the following questions:

- How does submitting to God and resisting the devil work together in the life of the believer?

- What does it mean that if we come near to God He will come near to us? (The more we seek God the more we will experience His presence in our lives.)

- How would you rephrase or explain "wash your hands, you sinners, and purify your hearts, you double-minded"?

Insight

Submit is a military term that refers to arranging in proper rank. It carries the meaning of responsible obedience for the good of everyone. It prevents confusion concerning who is leading the "charge." As believers, we submit to Christ and clear the way for the victory Christ promises.

▨ What are we supposed to grieve, mourn, and wail about?

▨ In what ways does God lift us up when we humble ourselves before Him?

In verses 11-12, James presents slander as a problem in the community of faith.

▨ What is slander?

▨ Who does James say the slanderer becomes according to verse 11? Why is this serious from God's perspective? What does it matter if what you say is true or not? (See Ephesians 4:2 and Titus 3:2.)

▨ Why is God the best judge of character, actions, and motives?

Invite someone to read James 4:13-17, then discuss the following,

There are three principles of life found in these verses:

1) God is in control (Verse 15 tells us to think of the future in terms of the Lord's will.)

2) Each day is a gift. (Ultimately all our days are in God's hands [v. 15].)

3) God will hold us accountable for future obedience. (Verse 17 tells us to do the good we ought to do.)

In light of these principles:

▨ How does James counsel us concerning our daily plans? How should we plan for the future?

▨ What is the overarching warning in these verses?

James is not speaking against goals and planning. He is teaching us to hold our plans lightly so that we are willing to change them or delay them to do God's bidding.

▨ How does a sense of self-reliance get in the way of submission to God about our plans?

▨ What does it mean to live with the mindset of "If it is the Lord's will, we will live and do this or that"?

▨ Where should we get direction and confirmation about our plans?

▨ How can we use the list from verses 7-10 to help us here?

James gives a definition of sin in verse 17.

▨ How would you interpret verse 17? (Sin is doing wrong. However, James tells us that sin is also not doing what is right.)

▨ What are examples of knowing the good you ought to do, but not doing it?

▨ In what ways can God helps us do the good we know we ought to do?

Connect to My Life and the World

The way to follow James' instructions and warning about pleasing God is to pray for clear discernment. Invite your group to get silent before God:

▨ Where are you most vulnerable to the pull of our culture?

▨ Who needs your positive words without judgment?

▨ How will you come near to God this week?

Close the prayer with a blessing by repeating John Wesley's words from the beginning.

Unit 2

The Message of James

May

14

ENDURANCE AND THE SECOND COMING

In light of Christ's return, the Christian community must remain missional.

THE WORD

JAMES 5:7-20

KEY VERSE

Be patient, then, brothers and sisters, until the Lord's coming. See how the farmer waits for the land to yield its valuable crop, patiently waiting for the autumn and spring rains. **8You too, be patient and stand firm, because the Lord's coming is near.** 9Don't grumble against one another, brothers and sisters, or you will be judged. The Judge is standing at the door!

10Brothers and sisters, as an example of patience in the face of suffering, take the prophets who spoke in the name of the Lord. 11As you know, we count as blessed those who have persevered. You have heard of Job's perseverance and have seen what the Lord finally brought about. The Lord is full of compassion and mercy.

12Above all, my brothers and sisters, do not swear—not by heaven or by earth or by anything else. All you need to say is a simple "Yes" or "No." Otherwise you will be condemned.

13Is anyone among you in trouble? Let them pray. Is anyone happy? Let them sing songs of praise. 14Is anyone among you sick? Let them call the elders of the church to pray over them and anoint them with oil in the name of the Lord. 15And the prayer offered in faith will make the sick person well; the Lord will raise them up. If they have sinned, they will be forgiven. 16Therefore confess your sins to each other and pray for each other so that you may be healed. The prayer of a righteous person is powerful and effective.

17Elijah was a human being, even as we are. He prayed earnestly that it would not rain, and it did not rain on the land for three and a half years. 18Again he prayed, and the heavens gave rain, and the earth produced its crops.

Last Week:

We understood we must not fail to do the good that we can do.

This Week:

We will understand our expectancy regarding the return of Christ.

¹⁹My brothers and sisters, if one of you should wander from the truth and someone should bring that person back, ²⁰remember this: Whoever turns a sinner from the error of their way will save them from death and cover over a multitude of sins.

ENGAGE THE WORD
PATIENCE!

James 5:7-12

James writes, "Be patient, then, brothers and sisters, until the Lord's coming. See how the farmer waits for the land to yield its valuable crop, patiently waiting for the autumn and spring rains" (5:7). Why does the farmer wait? Perhaps he/she has confidence in the faithfulness of the process because he/she knows that God is at work.

James continues, "You too, be patient and stand firm, because the Lord's coming is near" (5:8). Patience is grace! The entire Christian life depends upon patient grace. It is patient because the passage of time requires it. It is grace because of the promise of the presence of the Holy Spirit and the testimony of Scripture.

Jesus is coming again! This means that our entire life is seasoned by the knowledge and hope that the presence of God frames the future and, therefore, the present. It is a dire mistake to think the second coming is about looking out the window toward the eastern sky. While it is that, it is about how today unfolds in the providence of God.

James reminds his readers, "Don't grumble against one another, brothers and sisters, or you will be judged. The Judge is standing at the door" (5:9)! When we lose the frame of patient grace, it is easy to turn upon one another. Impatience arises at the point of the despair that often accompanies faithlessness.

On the other hand, patience reveals a calm embrace of the future as grace. Patient grace guards against the presumption of the future as a projection of our achievement. The point James seems to be making is that when we take our eyes off life in Christ,

🔊 **Listen:**

FoundryLeader.com: This week's *Illustrated Bible Life* "Article Out Loud" surveys how healing has been perceived by the church since the first Christian centuries.

Notes:

_____

_____

_____

_____

_____

_____

_____

_____

_____

_____

_____

_____

_____

_____

_____

_____

_____

Did You Know?
The word used for facing suffering in verse 10 appears only here in the New Testament. Its meaning ranges from disappointment to more extreme challenges that require the best we have to endure them.

PRAYER AND PATIENT GRACE

we look at others with disdain instead of objects of God's redeeming love. The future is not our work; it is God's call. James makes a sober plea, "Above all, my brothers and sisters, do not swear—not by heaven or by earth or by anything else. All you need to say is a simple 'Yes' or 'No.' Otherwise you will be condemned" (5:12). We do not need to swear at all because our faith is in the Lordship of Christ. When we are able to do this, we stand in the company of those who walk with the same blessed hope!

Patient grace enables us to endure: "Brothers and sisters, as an example of patience in the face of suffering, take the prophets who spoke in the name of the Lord. As you know, we count as blessed those who have persevered. You have heard of Job's perseverance and have seen what the Lord finally brought about. The Lord is full of compassion and mercy" (5:10-11). By any measure, people these days are fragile. It may be the pace of life or the many voices calling out to us as our life unfolds, but all the same, endurance may seem out of reach. Only when patient grace prevails can we follow the advice of James.

James 5:13-20

Prayer is a practice near and dear to patient grace. James writes, "And the prayer offered in faith will make the sick person well; the Lord will raise them up. If they have sinned, they will be forgiven. Therefore confess your sins to each other and pray for each other so that you may be healed" (5:15-16a). We practice patient hope by praying. Put another way, prayer is what people with patient hope do in times of stress and disappointment. Why is this so? Prayer names the reality of God in the midst of the storm as a sign of hope. The gospel tells us that God entered history to fight the battle we could never win in order to deliver us. James reminds his readers, "The prayer of a righteous person is powerful and effective" (5:16b). What makes the prayer of the righteous powerful and

Discover:

The Christian church throughout its history has affirmed the power of God to heal physical and emotional illness through non-medical, miraculous means. Yet healing ministry in the church today little resembles the types of healings we seen in the Gospels and Acts. Why has Christian understanding of healings changed throughout history? This week's *Illustrated Bible Life* article takes a closer look at "Healing and Holiness."

Notes:

Think About It

Jürgen Moltmann, an important theologian, reminds us that hope is rarely for the victor. Rather, it is for the poor and defeated. Because we know that Jesus is coming again, we can endure whatever challenges we face.

effective? Patient grace. Those who confidently know Christ are powerful to the extent that they lean into the "amazing grace" of God.

Patient grace opens life to the transcendent reality of God. For too many in our time, it is all up to us. I build my life, marriage, career, family, and future based on my rationality and persistence. This is the point where James has a word for us: "Elijah was a human being, even as we are. He prayed earnestly that it would not rain, and it did not rain on the land for three and a half years. Again he prayed, and the heavens gave rain, and the earth produced its crops" (5:17-18). Elijah was just a man, but he prayed. Patient grace fills our imagination with the possibilities of a world that is always more than we can see.

When suffering comes, we endure by the patient grace of a people made new in Christ. The Holy Spirit empowers those who follow Christ to embody patient grace that endures. Christians face the challenges presented in life, but they do not necessarily need to defeat us. James reminds us that Jesus is coming. There is an end to all of this if we endure in patient grace. At this point, patient grace comes clearly into view.

REFLECT Pray, asking God to help you develop patience in the face of suffering.

HENRY SPAULDING, II

Discussion Guide

Connect to My Experience

Bring a seed packet to your session and a small pot with dirt. Introduce today's session by explaining that James compares waiting for Christ's return to waiting for something to grow. Then, plant a few seeds in the pot and ask the following questions:

- How long will it take for us to see what will come up?

- What should we do while we wait? (tasks like watering, giving it sun, keeping pests away, and so on)

Remind everyone that God's Word reminds us that we are in a waiting period now. But that doesn't mean we don't have anything to do.

Transition:

James reminds us today that while we are in a waiting period for Christ's return, we have work to do until He does.

Connect to the Word

Invite someone to read James 5:7-12, then discuss the following,

The first admonition James gives us about the return of Christ is to learn how to wait patiently.

- How does James illustrate the kind of patience believers should have as we wait for the Lord to return? Why is this a good illustration of patience in the life of a believer?

In verses 8-10, James describes what patient waiting looks like and what does not belong.

- What action helps us refine our patience?

- What does James mean when he tells us to "stand firm because the Lord's coming is near"?

- Why does James warn against "grumbling against one another" in verse 9?

- What makes patience and perseverance difficult when connected to suffering? (v. 10)

James is speaking to scattered Christians who had to leave their homes to escape persecution.

- Considering this, what encouragement does James give in verse 11?

James reminds us in verse 12 that our speech should be truthful forthright.

- What does James mean by saying all we need to say is a "simple 'Yes' or 'No'"? (Our words should be trustworthy. When we avoid lies, half-truths, and omissions of truth we will be seen as a trustworthy person.)

- What role does the Holy Spirit play in our lives in communicating God's truth in and through us?

Invite someone to read James 5:13-20, then discuss the following,

Unexpected trouble makes it difficult to wait patiently for God to act. James wants to help us remember how to face trouble to strengthen our testimony and our patience.

- What are we supposed to do if we face trouble or experience blessing? (Pray and sing songs of praise.)

We are to pray for the sick and those in need of forgiveness.

- What should they/we do if a person is sick?

- Why should we pray for those who have sinned? What does that look like?

Insight

■ What is a prayer of faith and how is it focused?

■ Why does James connect healing to forgiveness in verse 15? (Soul sickness, which is spiritual failure, needs healing as well.)

■ What practice are we supposed to embrace as described in verse 16? (He is not suggesting "hanging out our dirty laundry" for everyone to see. However, he is suggesting that when a person has wronged someone, he/she must confess that failure to the one he/she has wronged. But, in some situations it may include public confession before the body and corporate prayer for that person.)

■ In what ways is the prayer of the righteous "powerful and effective"? (The righteous are committed to God and pray for His will to be accomplished.)

Elijah told the people that God said it would not rain, and it didn't. Then on Mt. Carmel, when God's integrity was on the line, Elijah prayed, and it rained heavily (1 Kings 17:1).

■ Did Elijah's prayer direct God or did God direct Elijah's prayer?

■ What is the lesson for us?

James reminds us that the stakes are high for someone who has "wandered from the truth" considering the second coming of Christ.

■ How should we pray for a person who has lost the way to God or hasn't found it yet? Why is this urgent work before Christ's return?

God saves, but He calls us to be involved in the life of those who have turned away from God.

■ What does it mean that if we help a sinner turn from the error of his or her way, we save him/her from death? (When a person repents and turns his/her life over to God, he/she is lead from spiritual death to spiritual life. See 1 Corinthians 11:30 and 1 John 5:16.)

■ How does leading a person to Christ "cover over a multitude of sins"? (When a person seeks God's forgiveness, every sin is forgiven, the entire quantity of his/her sins [Psalm 32:1]. God is fully aware of all our sin and Christ' sacrifice on the cross covers them all. See Luke 24:46-47.)

Connect to My Life and the World

James ends by talking about prayer as a priority for persevering patience while we wait for Christ's return.

■ How is our church a praying community?

■ What is one way that we could increase our prayer power?

Invite the group to think of people they know who need to find or return to God. Then pray:

■ That each person hears and receives God's Truth.

■ That each person recognize the life and death implications of his/her choices.

■ That the right person will come into their lives with the right words from God.

Close in prayer.

Unit 3

The Holy Spirit

Session Outcome

To help people understand and experience the fullness of the Holy Spirit as the enabler of Christian faith and growth.

Customize:

Spirit is the password to access expanded teaching helps on FoundryLeader.com.

Discover:

Illustrated Bible Life examines the person and work of the Holy Spirit, and provides verse-by-verse commentary on the Scripture passage.

May

21

WHO IS THE HOLY SPIRIT?

Jesus promises His presence, both now and forever.

THE WORD

JOHN 14:15-27

If you love me, keep my commands. ¹⁶And I will ask the Father, and he will give you another advocate to help you and be with you forever— ¹⁷the Spirit of truth. The world cannot accept him, because it neither sees him nor knows him. But you know him, for he lives with you and will be in you. ¹⁸I will not leave you as orphans; I will come to you. ¹⁹Before long, the world will not see me anymore, but you will see me. Because I live, you also will live. ²⁰On that day you will realize that I am in my Father, and you are in me, and I am in you. ²¹Whoever has my commands and keeps them is the one who loves me. The one who loves me will be loved by my Father, and I too will love them and show myself to them."

²²Then Judas (not Judas Iscariot) said, "But, Lord, why do you intend to show yourself to us and not to the world?"

²³Jesus replied, "Anyone who loves me will obey my teaching. My Father will love them, and we will come to them and make our home with them. ²⁴Anyone who does not love me will not obey my teaching. These words you hear are not my own; they belong to the Father who sent me.

KEY VERSE ²⁵"All this I have spoken while still with you. **²⁶But the Advocate, the Holy Spirit, whom the Father will send in my name, will teach you all things and will remind you of everything I have said to you.** ²⁷Peace I leave with you; my peace I give you. I do not give to you as the world gives. Do not let your hearts be troubled and do not be afraid.

Last Week:

We explored the importance of Christian living in light of Christ's return.

This Week:

We will explore the promise Jesus makes to His disciples regarding the gift of the Holy Spirit and the implications this has for our faith journey with the Lord.

Session 12

ENGAGE THE WORD

Jesus told the disciples that He was leaving them, and they were stunned and scared. He was going back to heaven to the Father. With Him gone, what were they going to do? What was going to happen to them? How would they thrive without a leader, a master teacher, like Jesus? We will see how He comforted them with three promises.

JESUS PROMISES THE SPIRIT

John 14:15-19

The promise of the Spirit goes back at least 500 years before Jesus to the prophet Ezekiel: "I will give you a new heart and put a new spirit in you.... And I will put my Spirit in you and move you to follow my decrees and be careful to keep my laws" (36:26-27). This encouraged the Jews of that day that God had not left them forever in exile in Babylon and would relate to them in a deeper way than through human kings, prophets, laws, and regulations. A new heart, a new human spirit, and the Holy Spirit would mean a new day of holy behavior unknown from Adam and Eve until then. Jesus' promise of the Holy Spirit was the fulfillment of the promise of the Father centuries ago. That's why Jesus emphasizes obedience and connects it to the coming of the Holy Spirit, the Spirit of truth (John 14:15-17, 21, 23-24). The Holy Spirit's role is to lead Christians into holy living; this is a major part of the gospel. The good news is that God has saved us to sanctify us!

JESUS PROMISES INTIMACY

John 14:20-24

Another connection Jesus makes is between obedience and love. Those who obey Jesus are those who love Him. Also, to those who love Him, Jesus gives the promise of intimacy: "You will realize that I am in my Father, and you are in me, and I am in you" (John 14:20). Ever since Adam and Eve lost true intimacy with God and each other due to their sin, all people (whether knowingly or not) have longed for intimacy with God and with each other. John, the disciple, built

▶ **Watch:**

Dr. Roger Hahn introduces this unit on the Holy Spirit.

🔊 **Listen:**

FoundryLeader.com: This week's *Illustrated Bible Life* "Article Out Loud" traces the Holy Spirit from the Old Testament to the New Testament.

Notes:

_____

_____

_____

_____

_____

_____

_____

_____

_____

_____

_____

_____

_____

_____

_____

_____

_____

_____

_____

Did You Know?

The word "Advocate" (Greek: *parakletos*; English: "paraklaytos") can also be translated comforter, counselor, intercessor. Jesus used the adjective, "another," not to mean "different," but to assure His disciples that the Holy Spirit is another counselor exactly like Jesus.

on this later in his first epistle: "So that you also may have fellowship with us. And our fellowship is with the Father and with His Son, Jesus Christ" (1 John 1:3). With the Holy Spirit resident in each believer, God's love, joy, peace, friendship, companionship, warnings, forgiveness, strength, assurance, encouragement, and so on all became available to the Christian mind and spirit. This is the natural outflow of the ministry of Jesus, the next step after the crucifixion, resurrection, and ascension. Pentecost, when the Holy Spirit descended upon the disciples, brought direct fellowship between God and His people in a way never before.

God created us as relational beings. During the COVID-19 pandemic came protocols of handwashing, mask-wearing, and physical distancing. Staying at home rather than going to the store, restaurant, school, or the office for over a year led to painful feelings of separation. God desires that we be in close relationship with Him. Through the presence of the Holy Spirit, we can draw near to God (James 4:8) and experience intimacy with Him (John 15:4-6). God also desires that we exhibit Christlikeness in our relationship with others (family, friends, co-workers, and so on). Through the Holy Spirit true intimacy with others is made possible. What a joy!

JESUS PROMISES TEACHING

John 14:25-27

Jesus is known as the master teacher. He knew His audience and used examples from agriculture and powerful stories to communicate truths about God, humans, and salvation. He taught the multitude about the kingdom of God and ran circles around the self-exalted teachers of Israel, the scribes, and Pharisees. Also, His disciples benefitted by living, eating, and ministering every day for three years with Him. He answered their questions and even questioned them as a teaching method. Imagine how great it would be to hear revelation from Jesus himself any day of the week!

 **Discover:**

In many respects, John 14—17 is the high watermark of teaching regarding the Spirit in the New Testament. In order to see John's distinctive contribution clearly, we must go back to the Old Testament and the other works of the New Testament. In this week's *Illustrated Bible Life* article, "The Holy Spirit," we'll take a closer look at the appearance of the Spirit throughout the Scriptures.

Think About It

The world system cannot accept the Holy Spirit because it neither sees Him nor knows Him. We Christians, however, have the Holy Spirit in us (v.17). God himself makes His home in us!

Even better, a greater opportunity is ours today within us through the Holy Spirit! "The Advocate, the Holy Spirit,...will teach you all things and remind you of everything that I have said to you" (John 14:26). Notice that the role of the Holy Spirit is not to speak His own words (John 14:10, 25), but to remind us of Jesus' words and lead us into all the truth (John 16:13-15). On top of that, the presence of the Holy Spirit is ours forever (John 14:16)!

One of my favorite public high school English teachers put up on the classroom bulletin board a single phrase: "Everything costs." That so struck me as a huge truth in so few words. I have never forgotten it from over 40 years ago. A single thought can change our lives. When Jesus says that the Holy Spirit will lead us into all the truth, we learn from both Spirit-anointed words of Scripture and from the Spirit's truth received into our very spirit, soul, and body. The Spirit and the Bible always agree, so what a privilege for us to experience Him!

The Holy Spirit, the third person of the Trinity, is crucial to the Christian life. Through abiding in each Christian through the Holy Spirit, Jesus can do more than if He stayed on earth in human form. Jesus promises 1) His followers holiness through the enablement of the Holy Spirit, 2) Spirit-enabled intimacy between God and the believer, and 3) the truth from God through the Holy Spirit's teaching.

REFLECT Do you feel Jesus' presence and hear Him through the Holy Spirit?

JOSEPH AUGELLO is adjunct professor at Mount Vernon Nazarene University (Bible, Theology, Ethics), ordained elder in the Church of the Nazarene, and former pastor of three Nazarene and other Wesleyan-Holiness Churches.

Notes:

_____

_____

_____

_____

_____

_____

_____

_____

_____

_____

_____

_____

_____

_____

_____

_____

Discussion Guide

Connect to My Experience

We've all learned lessons in life. Some have had a bigger impact on us than others. Lead your group in a discussion recalling lessons they remember from their school days.

- What was the most memorable lesson you were taught as a young student in elementary school, junior high, high school, or college?

- What is the most important life lesson you ever learned?

- How did you learn the lesson and what do you remember about the one who taught you? How have you passed that lesson on to others?

Transition:

Today we will study when God the Son points to the sending of the Holy Spirit to be a powerful presence in the life of believers.

Connect to the Word

Invite someone to read John 14:15-19, then discuss the following,

Jesus was teaching from the upper room just after the Last Supper. Judas had left to betray Him, but Jesus was encouraging His friends and disciples who may have been afraid or discouraged by Christ's recent words about His pending sufferings.

- What did Jesus say would be the evidence of their love for Him? (They were to continue to follow—live in obedience to—what He had taught them and have fellowship with Him.)

Jesus is our first advocate (1 John 2:1). In response to their loving obedience, Christ promised "another advocate to help" and be with them "forever."

- How does the promise of "forever" bring us hope? (The Holy Spirit is continually with us for always.)

- In what ways is the Holy Spirit "the Spirit of truth"? (He guides Christ-followers into all truth.)

- Why can't the world "accept Him"? (This does not mean those in the world cannot become believers. It does mean that those who trust and obey Jesus, return His love, and cease to be part of the world—born anew of the Spirit.)

- What is the promise to the disciples in verse 18? How does this remain a promise for us today?

- What do you think Jesus meant by "Because I live, you will also live"? (Believers have passed from death to life because of the death and resurrection of Jesus. See 1 Corinthians 15:19-20.)

- How do you think the disciples felt after hearing Christ's words in verses 18-19? What was the hopeful message Jesus was giving them (and us)?

Invite someone to read John 14:20-24, then discuss the following,

The link Jesus makes between the believer's obedience and intimacy with the Father is amazing. God desires intimacy, which we see in the life of Christ and the presence of the Holy Spirit. The evidence of that love is reciprocated in the obedience of the believer.

- In what ways does God make His home in believers?

- How does a believer realize the extent of God's residence in their heart? (When we allow God's Spirit to work in and through our lives.)

- According to verse 21, what does Jesus reveal about God's love when a

Insight

believer keeps Christ's commands and loves Him? (The correlation between their love of God and the Father's love and Christ's love for them.)

- How does Jesus describe the level of God's intimacy with obedient believers in verse 23? (They make their home with them.)

A person who loves Jesus will obey His teaching.

- Why does obedience express our love of and trust in Jesus? (God's love is not dependent on my obedience. But if we truly love Jesus, we live to obey and follow Him.)

- Why do you think Jesus felt it so important in this, His last group lesson before His arrest, to connect obedience to His commands and the gift of "the Spirit of Truth"?

Invite someone to read John 14:25-27, then discuss the following,

Jesus knew that they were facing a season of fear soon. So, He encouraged them with a promise that the Holy Spirit would teach them and He would give them peace.

- What name does Jesus give to the Holy Spirit describing His upcoming roles?

- What is the Holy Spirit's responsibility according to Jesus? (advocate, teach, and remind)

- In what ways are "teaching" and "reminding" crucial for our faith journey?

- What encouragement does Jesus leave with His disciples? (v. 27)

- What's the difference between how Jesus gives peace and the peace the world offers? (motives, costs, and effects are different)

- From what we have read and discussed today, how is Jesus' words, "Do not let your hearts be troubled and do not be afraid," a source hope and comfort?

Connect to My Life and the World

The Spirit's presence in our lives today is Christ's kept promise of the Holy Spirit making His home in the hearts of believers. The Holy Spirit teaches and reminds us of the truths Christ taught His disciples.

- Why is it important to remember that Christ's promises to the apostles also apply to believers today?

- How would your faith journey be different without the presence of the Holy Spirit in your life?

- What effect does the Holy Spirit have on your daily life?

- How is your faith in Christ affected by the promises Christ made and kept?

Because Christ made and kept His promise to ask the Father to send us the Holy Spirit, we can put our faith in His words, His teachings, and His actions. The Spirit is with us. He is comforting us, sustaining us, sanctifying us, and reminding us of the truths of God.

Close your session with prayer.

Sessions 12-13 are written by Chad Garinger

Chad has been a Nazarene pastor for 30 years, currently serving the Lord in Portsmouth, Ohio with his wife and two teenage children.

Unit 3

The Holy Spirit

May
28

PENTECOST

The indwelling of the Holy Spirit empowers the believer for holy living and obedient service.

THE WORD

ACTS 2:1-4   When the day of Pentecost came, they were all together in one place. ²Suddenly a sound like the blowing of a violent wind came from heaven and filled the whole house where they were sitting. ³They saw what seemed to be tongues of fire that separated and came to rest on each of them. ⁴All of them were filled with the Holy Spirit and began to speak in other tongues as the Spirit enabled them.

17-18   ¹⁷"'In the last days, God says, I will pour out my Spirit on all people. Your sons and daughters will prophesy, your young men will see visions, your old men will dream dreams.

¹⁸Even on my servants, both men and women, I will pour out my Spirit in those days, and they will prophesy.

38-39
KEY VERSE   **³⁸Peter replied, "Repent and be baptized, every one of you, in the name of Jesus Christ for the forgiveness of your sins. And you will receive the gift of the Holy Spirit. ³⁹The promise is for you** and your children and for all who are far off—for all whom the Lord our God will call."

10:44-48   ⁴⁴While Peter was still speaking these words, the Holy Spirit came on all who heard the message. ⁴⁵The circumcised believers who had come with Peter were astonished that the gift of the Holy Spirit had been poured out even on Gentiles. ⁴⁶For they heard them speaking in tongues and praising God.

Then Peter said, ⁴⁷"Surely no one can stand in the way of their being baptized with water. They have received the Holy Spirit just as

Last Week:

We examined the work and ministry of the Holy Spirit.

This Week:

We will examine the meaning of the Spirit-filled life.

Session 13

we have." ⁴⁸So he ordered that they be baptized in the name of Jesus Christ. Then they asked Peter to stay with them for a few days.

ENGAGE THE WORD

After Jesus ascended back to heaven, the disciples and other followers of Jesus obeyed His instructions and waited and prayed together for 10 days. All of sudden, the most amazing experience of the Holy Spirit overwhelmed them and changed them forever. We will make three observations about that day and what we can learn from it.

Acts 2:1-4

The promise of the pouring out of the Holy Spirit on all people (Joel 2:28) was realized in the historical event of Pentecost. Ten days earlier, on the day He went back to heaven, Jesus told His disciples to wait for the Holy Spirit, "Do not leave Jerusalem, but wait for the gift my Father promised, which you heard me speak about. For John baptized with water, but in a few days you will be baptized with the Holy Spirit" (Acts 1:4b-5).

THE EXPERIENCE WAS HISTORIC

In the Old Testament days, God's Spirit anointed specific leaders for a mission (Moses, Samson, Saul, David, Solomon, the prophets), but it was only the few, not the whole Israelite nation. Jesus promised that the Holy Spirit (the Advocate) would be sent (John 16:13-14); not only would the Holy Spirit come, but those who received the Holy Spirit would receive power (Acts 1:8). This promise was fulfilled at Pentecost. From that day until now, God's Spirit has been poured out on all those (Acts 15:8-9) who will open their hearts by faith to the Holy Spirit's working in their lives.

At Pentecost the goal of the gospel was accomplished—forgiveness, adoption into the family of God, and receiving the power from on high to enable consistent obedience to God's Word and mission through the Holy Spirit. Since this historic event, believers have been experiencing God's transforming work of

Listen:

FoundryLeader.com: The diaspora of the Jews in the centuries leading up to Christ's incarnation is the focus of this week's *Illustrated Bible Life* "Article Out Loud."

Notes:

_____

_____

_____

_____

_____

_____

_____

_____

_____

_____

_____

_____

_____

_____

_____

_____

_____

Did You Know?

"Pentecost" (Greek, *pentecoste*; English: "petaykostay") means fiftieth. The Jewish festival which celebrated the Law of God 50 days after the Passover. God sent the Holy Spirit on this day to make wholehearted, consistent obedience possible.

THE EXPERIENCE WAS COMMUNAL

THE EXPERIENCE WAS PERSONAL

holiness in their lives through the last 2,000 years of church history.

Acts 2:17-18, 38-39

This happened in a community of 120 in the upper room and turned the church into a much larger community. Since all of the group of believers received the Holy Spirit, this points to the new community of God. No one is left out. Further, to celebrate Pentecost (occurring 50 days after Passover), a huge annual number of Jews and Jewish converts had traveled from other towns and nations. The disciples witnessed to these people during this event. Some who did not understand this event accused the disciples of being drunk because they spoke in languages not their own to the crowds.

Then Peter announced to the visitors that they were not drunk. This event was God's plan all along for the last days, to pour out His Spirit on all people. He quoted the prophet Joel about this event (Acts 2:17-18, 21). Peter's point was that this was a miracle from God through Jesus, the Messiah: "God has raised this Jesus to life.... Exalted to the right hand of God, He has received from the Father the promised Holy Spirit and has poured out what you see and hear" (Acts 2:32-33). As a result, about 3,000 people believed in Jesus and joined the new community of God (Acts 2:41)! This is one of the roles of the Holy Spirit, to save and sanctify and bring believers together into the new community!

Acts 10:44-48

After Pentecost, as Peter preached to a large gathering of Gentiles at Cornelius' house, the Holy Spirit came upon everyone (each person) who heard the message.

Peter explained to the Jerusalem visitors (2:38-39) once they were convicted in their hearts that Jesus was the true Messiah, they needed to "repent and be baptized" in the name of Jesus Christ for the forgive-

Discover:

The book of Acts records that there were many devout Jews in Jerusalem to celebrate Pentecost when the Holy Spirit first descended upon the early Christians. Acts records that these Jewish onlookers reported being from more than a dozen areas. Why were so many Jewish believers spread out around the known world of the time? This week's *Illustrated Bible Life* article, "The Diaspora," explains.

Notes:

Think About It

The word, "baptize" (Greek, *baptizo*, English: "baptidzo") means to overwhelm or immerse. This means to be totally drowned in the Holy Spirit. This had never happened corporately among God's people before Pentecost.

ness of their sins. Then they would receive the gift of the Holy Spirit. The implication is that the crowd consisted of Jews and Jewish converts that needed to be saved. We see that those both in Jerusalem and Caesarea (in the house of Cornelius, Acts 10:44-48) decided to believe individually in Jesus, and the Holy Spirit came upon them all. From this point forward, their lives would never be the same.

At Pentecost God poured His Holy Spirit out on those who were open and receptive to the Holy Spirit's infilling. Every generation from the early church until today has testified to God's call to holy living and empowerment by His Spirit to transform their lives into the likeness of Christ. The work of the Holy Spirit transforms us both in a moment and over our lifetime. But this transformational work is not a one-way relationship. Our love and dedication for God moves us to fully surrender our lives to Him—dying out to self-control and self-centeredness.

Romans 12:1-2 says, "Therefore, I urge you, brothers and sisters, in view of God's mercy, to offer your bodies as a living sacrifice, holy and pleasing to God—this is your true and proper worship. Do not conform to the pattern of this world, but be transformed by the renewing of your mind. Then you will be able to test and approve what God's will is—his good, pleasing and perfect will." As we daily commit ourselves to God, God through the Holy Spirit transforms us into Christlikeness.

REFLECT Have you experienced the infilling of the Holy Spirit?

JOSEPH AUGELLO

Discussion Guide

Connect to My Experience

Every generation experiences at least one historically significant event that affects everyone. The event is often tragic, catastrophic, or technologically advanced. Almost all of us remember where we were when it happened.

◼ What was your generation's "I-remember-where-I-was-when" experience? Where were you when it happened?

(Examples: Pearl Harbor attack, D-Day, Kennedy assassination, first man on the moon, fall of Berlin wall, 9/11, natural disasters, and so on.)

◼ How did that historical event impact your community, family, and you personally?

Transition:

Today we will look at the experience those early believers who received the gift of the Holy Spirit.

Connect to the Word

Invite someone to read Acts 2:1-4, then discuss the following,

The story of the gift of the Holy Spirit is historical fact complete with witnesses and evidence that is still evident and relevant today.

◼ What do you notice about the scene of this historical event? People, places, timing? (The setting is the Jewish festival of Pentecost, occurring 50 days after Passover. There was a diverse crowd.)

Sound is reminiscent of God's appearance at Sinai (Exodus 19:16-19), wind symbolizes the Spirit of God (Ezekiel 37:9-14), and fire the presence of God (Exodus 3:2).

◼ What does this tell us about this movement of God upon the people?

◼ What does it say to you that the "tongues of fire" separated and rested on each of them? (Each person was filled with the Holy Spirit.)

This would have been an amazing experience.

◼ Share a time when you saw and/or experienced the moving of the Holy Spirit in an amazing way.

Invite someone to read Acts 2:17-18, 38-39, then discuss the following,

The crowd, seeing all this, thought they were drunk. But Peter assures them they are not (v. 15).

◼ In what ways can people misunderstand the moving of the Holy Spirit in a believer's life?

Peter quotes an 850 year old prophecy of Joel (2:28), who is quoting God, proving the relevance of Scripture.

◼ What is the message of this prophecy? (God has promised to pour out His Spirit on all people.)

◼ How was this prophecy fulfilled then in Acts? In what ways have you seen this prophecy being fulfilled today?

◼ By quoting Joel, what was his message to the crowd? (Joel's prophecy was being fulfilled before their eyes. The crowd was not seeing the actions of drunkards, but the moving of the Holy Spirit.)

Peter preaches to the crowd telling them about Jesus.

◼ What did Peter challenge the observers to do in response to his sermon and all they were witnessing? (Repent and be baptized.)

Insight

Through the life-giving work of the Holy Spirit, God can transform our lives and make us more and more like Jesus, the one who did not consider equality with God something to be used to His own advantage; rather, He made himself nothing (Philippians 2:6-7).

■ Why do you think his message was so brief, yet so powerful?

■ How does Peter's message inform the church of its message? (We are to reach out to the world in love with the message of redemption.)

■ How did Peter's challenge/offer expand the reach of the community of believers? (Having been told by Jesus that they were going to be His witnesses "to the ends of the earth" in Acts 1:8, Peter was passing on that truth by prophetic faith.)

Just after giving this plea and a warning, about 3,000 were added to their number (v. 41).

■ What lessons could be gleaned from Peter's address to the believers and then to those who were observing and listening to them?

Invite someone to read Acts 10:44-48, then discuss the following,

[Read verses 24-27, or share with the group that these verses take place at the house of Cornelius.]

Believers are those who have turned from their sin and placed their faith in God, convinced by the gospel by the will of the Father and the power and presence of the Holy Spirit. When they choose to put their faith in the salvation Christ's life, death and resurrection provide, it is so by the work of the Holy Spirit in them. That work is personal. It is corporate inasmuch as it is for the whole world, but it is individuals who choose salvation and sanctification.

■ What happened to the Gentiles when Peter told them the gospel message? What was the evidence?

■ When the Spirit came on the Gentiles, what changed in Peter and eventually the other believers? (Gentiles were baptized, making them equal in the eyes of the Jewish believers.)

■ Do we ever find ourselves surprised by the power of gospel working in the lives of others? If so, what do these passages remind us of the reach of the gospel and the power of the Holy Spirit?

Connect to My Life and the World

Today we have seen the power of the gospel message and the pouring out of the Holy Spirit.

■ What are some of the most important spiritual events of your life so far? Why?

■ Share about your experience of when you made the choice to receive God's forgiveness (salvation).

■ Share about your experience of the infilling of the Holy Spirit (entire sanctification) and the difference that choice made in your life.

Being sanctified means totally consecrating, or giving full control of, our lives to God. When we allow the Holy Spirit full reign in our lives, we grow in faith and become more Christlike in thought and character.

Invite your group to get silent before God. Then ask,

■ Have you invited God to take up residence in your life?

■ Are there areas of your life that you have not given God full control over?

■ What areas of your life would you like to surrender to God's Spirit today?

Close your session with prayer.

MATERIALS AVAILABLE

For the leader:

Leader's Guide—one for each leader and assistant leader.

Illustrated Bible Life—background articles/commentary; one for each leader and assistant leader.

Bible Teaching Maps—one for each group.

For the adult participant:

Bible Study Guide—one for each adult in your group. (Also available in large print.)

Standard—take-home Christian leisure-reading magazine; one for each adult.

Reflecting God—daily devotions based on scriptures and themes found in *Adult Faith Connections.* One per household. (Also available in large print.)

Mike L. Wonch
    Editor
Judi King
    Editor, *Illustrated Bible Life*
Bonnie J. Perry
    Director of Editorial
Mark D. Brown
    Publisher

A Year at a Glance . . .

SUMMER 2023

Unit 1: Holy Living

This unit explores what it truly means to live a life growing each day in Christ-likeness.

Unit 2: Hard Sayings of the Old Testament

When reading the Old Testament, we sometimes encounter passages that seem confusing. In this unit, we will look closer at passages that challenge our understanding of God and Scripture.

Unit 3: Titus and Philemon

This unit looks at two letters of Paul. We will examine the letter Paul sent Titus, instructing him about faith and conduct. We will also examine the letter Paul sent to Philemon and the members of the church at Colossae.

FALL 2023

Unit 1: Lessons from the Kings of Judah

The kings of Judah were powerful and influential. Some were good, and others not-so-good. We will examine the lessons learned from these leaders.

Unit 2: The Message of Ezekiel

God revealed himself to Ezekiel in many wonderful ways. In this study, we will explore these encounters and discover what they teach us about God.

WINTER 2023-24

Unit 1: A Savior is Born

Celebrate the birth of Jesus by contemplating on the extraordinary stories leading up to the Messiah's coming, culminating in the Savior's entering the world as a baby in a manger.

Unit 2: The Parables of Jesus in Luke

Jesus used simple, but relatable stories to teach important spiritual lessons for our daily lives. This unit looks at many of the parables Jesus taught from the book of Luke.

SPRING 2024

Unit 1: 1 Corinthians

In this study, we will see how Paul addresses the problems between the Corinthian believers through the light of the gospel message.

Unit 2: 2 Corinthians

In this study, Paul addresses such issues as suffering, forgiveness, reflecting God's glory, and being generous.

Lightning Source UK Ltd.
Milton Keynes UK
UKHW052013301222
414662UK00007B/91